M000235462

The

BLESSED

Life

*Enjoying Life in the Kingdom
from the 'Sermon on the Mount'
Perspective*

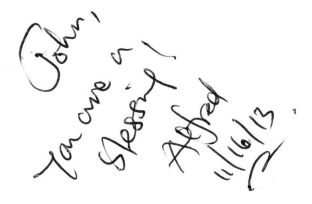

John,
Tan cure a
Blessing!
Alfred
11/16/13

The Blessed Life

The
BLESSED
Life

Enjoying Life In The Kingdom From The "Sermon On The Mount" Perspective

Alfred Tagoe

The BLESSED Life
Alfred Tagoe

ISBN: 978-0615843742

Copyright © 2013 by Voice of Revival Ministries

All rights reserved. No part of this book may be reproduced or transmitted in any form or by any means without written permission from the author.

Voice of Revival Ministries
5696 Earnings Dr,
Columbus, OH, 43232.
www.voiceofrevival.net

Printed in the United States of America

Unless otherwise noted, all Scripture is taken from the New King James Version copyright © 1982 Thomas Nelson, Inc. Used by permission. All rights reserved.
*Scripture text in bold or italics is the emphasis of the author.

This book is dedicated to the loving memories of Wing Commander Eddie Tagoe, my late natural father; and Wing Commander (Dr) Sam Annankra, my late spiritual father. Both these men have been instrumental in shaping who I am today. I also dedicate this book to all fathers, both natural and spiritual, whose examples in the Lord continue to shape the lives of the ones God has placed under their care. Well done!

CONTENTS

ACKNOWLEDGEMENT

I first want to acknowledge my co-author, the precious Holy Spirit, whose insight and inspiration guided the production of the contents of this book. To my loving wife, Angie, whose love and support continues to encourage me I say "thank you". Many thanks go to Evelyn Turnbull who helped to edit this book. Her expertise is always invaluable.

I would like to acknowledge and thank my many mentors through whom God has used to instruct, inspire, and motivate me in my divine quest to know and please God: Eastwood Anaba, Michael Botchway, Ekow Eshun, Steve & Stanley Mensah, Rod Parsley, Brondon Mathis, and James Dixon. In addition, to all my friends and ministry partners world-wide, I say "thank you" for your friendship and support. Furthermore to my CoHOP family, words alone cannot express my sincere gratitude for your labor of love that you have displayed as we build His House of Prayer together. Finally, to Mike Bickle of the International House of Prayer whose teaching and insight on this and many subjects has been a tremendous blessing and inspiration to pursue God with all my heart and strength.

May the Lord cause His countenance to shine over all of you.

ENDORSEMENTS

The Blessed Life is a writing that empowers the reader with the basic premise of the Kingdom, that is, to create a lifestyle that mirrors that of Jesus Christ on the earth. Alfred introduces the reader to a new awareness of how to proceed in life with the empowerment of the "blessing." Melchizedek blessed Abraham. *The Blessed Life* will provide principles of Kingdom living that will offer the reader the opportunity to engage in the same great exchange. Upon reading and studying the Blessed Life the reader can be assured of a Kingdom life-style that will empower them in authority, increase and winning strategies in life."

Louis F. Kayatin D.D. D.M.
Senior Pastor,
Church on the North Coast, Lorain, Ohio

I first met Alfred in 2011, at a "Onething Regional Conference" we were hosting in Wilmington, Ohio. Little did I know that first meeting would grow into a friendship of mutual respect and admiration as we began to journey together as House of Prayer leaders in the state of Ohio. I can confidently say that Alfred embodies the Sermon on the Mount lifestyle and teaches it from experience; expounding on the beatitudes in a way I've seen few teachers do, such as, Meekness: Strength under Control, and Purity: Your Divine Power Source. He deals candidly, and pulls no punches in challenging us, the Church, to examine our hearts and mindsets against the truths of the beatitudes. Using comparisons and analogies from Jesus to David and from horses to donkeys, you'll find the author's insight compelling you to read more! *The Blessed Life* is more than just a book about the Sermon on the Mount, it's a book taking you into the heart of God's desire to prepare for Himself a people who rightly exemplify Him and the great rewards they'll encounter as each beatitude fashions them into a pure and spotless Bride made ready for Her soon and coming King.

Robyn Morris
Director,
Wilmington House of Prayer, Wilmington, Ohio

Again from a heart emblazoned with the passion to see the will of God done on earth, comes another classic. The exposition on the Beatitudes by our beloved brother will not only open your eyes fresh to the wonderful treasures that are already yours in Christ, but also empower you to access them. A blessed life is a life empowered by God to prosper in all things. This book is inspired by the Holy Spirit and placed in your hands that you may know how blessed you are, and how you may walk in your blessedness. Enjoy it.

Sam Adeyemi
Senior Pastor,
Overcomers Church Intl, Columbus, Ohio

Alfred Tagoe has done it! He has shared God's constitution for Life in the Sermon on the Mount. In these pages he empowers each of us to overcome, as he takes us step by step through these verses, teaching us to persevere by encountering God's revelation, love, and devotion for us. I not only recommend this book for your personal time but also for your small group or youth group.

Benjamin Atkinson,
Intercessory Missionary,
International House of Prayer (IHOP-KC)

PREFACE

BLESSED! It is one of the most common words used, especially among people of faith. In many cultures you may hear people saying: "I am blessed", "be blessed" or "God bless you". These phrases are heard frequently among Christians and even non-Christians worldwide. Its meaning and significance has been studied, written, and spoken about by clergy and laity alike. I believe it is one of the most popular subjects among congregants; and Preachers are most willing to oblige their hearers with sermons about "God's blessings". Are people just saying these phrases because it is a common thing to say? Do people really know what they are saying when they say the phrase; "God bless you?"

As stated earlier, many a theologian, teacher of the Word of God, Preacher, and even the ordinary Sunday Church Service attendee has either casually studied or put forward an in depth analysis of the subject "BLESSING" or "BLESSED". Many in the Church understand and accept the general meaning of the concept of "blessing" as simply the good things God generously bestows upon His children such as a good car, nice house, good clothes, enough money to take care of all their bills, food, favor on the job and relationships. Hence, it is not very surprising that one of the most popular responses when a Christian is asked about their welfare is: "I am BLESSED and highly favored." Others, however, put more emphasis on the spiritual aspects of what Jesus' death, burial, resurrection, and ascension purchased for the believer as the blessing;

such as healing, deliverance from divers demonic bondages such as oppression and depression, and the spiritual gifts He bestows on us in order to become effective witnesses of His resurrection.

Kenneth Copeland, one of the foremost authorities on the subject of "The Blessing", in my humble opinion, opines that the blessing is not so much the good things which we have and can see such as houses, cars, riches, good marriage, etc. which many in our society crave for; but instead it is the 'force' of God on the person who is in covenant with God$_1$. In other words, there is a spiritual force, as it were, on the person who understands the rights, privileges, and conditions of their covenant with God as a result of the finished work of Jesus Christ on the cross of Calvary. It is this "spiritual force" otherwise known as the "blessing" that produces the kind of lifestyle that we then judge as blessed. Put in another way, the houses, cars, good health, good marriage, good job, and riches are not necessarily the blessing, but rather products of the blessing. This is what Solomon, the richest and wisest man according to scripture, meant when he boldly declared in Proverbs 10:22.

Proverbs 10:22: *"The blessing of the LORD makes one rich, And He adds no sorrow with it"*

As the above scripture clearly states, it is the "blessing" that produces the "riches". Therefore, instead of seeking the fruit or product which is the "riches" or the "stuff", we need to focus more on seeking the source, root or force which is "the blessing" and it only comes when we understand our covenant rights and privileges... walking in obedience to God's commandments in His Word.

Isaiah 1:19: *"If you are willing and obedient, You shall eat the good of the land"*

In addition to the above explanations and exhortations concerning the blessing of God, I do believe that there is another facet of this subject that though incredibly expressed in the Bible, has been largely ignored by many teachers, preachers, and Christians at large. This facet of the blessing of God is the thrust of this book.

One of the most popular and used verses to support all the above suppositions about the blessing of God is Ephesians 1:3.

Ephesians 1:3: *"Blessed be the God and Father of our Lord Jesus Christ, who has blessed us with every spiritual blessing in the heavenly places in Christ"*

As we however take a closer look at the meaning of the words used in this verse in their original context, we begin to see another dimension of the meaning of the word "blessed" or "blessing" other than what most of us for so long have interpreted to mean. According to Strong's Dictionary of Greek and Hebrew words, "blessed" in the above verse is the Greek word "Eulogeo", where we get our English word "Eulogy" and it means: "to *speak well of,*

> BEING BLESSED MEANS YOU ARE WELL SPOKEN OF BY GOD

that is, (religiously) to *bless* (*thank* or *invoke a benediction upon, prosper*)"2.

In other words, being "blessed" means you are "well spoken of" by God! Granted that what God says becomes; hence, in so many respects this translates into what we have already defined as the blessing. However, the emphasis here is not what we perceive or see as the blessing, but what God is thinking and saying about us.

It is one thing for you to be eulogized by your favorite "idol" in life or even the greatest man or woman on earth; but it is a totally different thing for you to be "well spoken of" by the Creator of the Universe; God Himself.

Have You Considered My Servant Job?

To further explain the awesomeness of this thought; let's take a brief look at the life of one of the most "blessed" men in the Bible. Everyone will agree, including God and the devil, that Job was one of the most blessed and highly favored men of his generation. However, the nature of his blessing can be disputed: was he blessed because of all he had in possessions or was he blessed because of what God thought and spoke about him?

It is amazing that the day God opened His mouth to speak well of or rather bless Job, he lost everything he possessed. God's conversation with our arch enemy, Satan, concerning Job is revealing in that it exposes the different ways we interpret what the blessing is.

Job 1:6-12: *"Now there was a day when the sons of ⌣ came to present themselves before the LORD, and Satan also came among them. And the LORD said to Satan, "From where do you come?" So Satan answered the LORD and said, "From going to and fro on the earth, and from walking back and forth on it." Then the LORD said to Satan,* ***"Have you considered My servant Job, that*** *there is* ***none like him on the earth, a blameless and upright man, one who fears God and shuns evil?"*** *So Satan answered the LORD and said, "Does Job fear God for nothing? Have You not made a hedge around him, around his household, and around all that he has on every side?* ***You have blessed the work of his hands, and his possessions have increased in the land.*** *But now, stretch out Your hand and touch all that he has, and he will surely curse You to Your face!" And the LORD said to Satan, "Behold, all that he has is in your power; only do not lay a hand on his person." So Satan went out from the presence of the LORD"*

According to the devil (and unfortunately some Christians agree,) from verse 9-11, Job's "blessing" was related to the things God had given him such as sound protection, abundant provision; and hence power and influence in society, (**see Job 29**). The devil also concluded that the reason Job feared God was because of these 'blessings' God had procured for him. In other words, just like many people today, the devil thought that Job was a blessed man and a good person who feared God because of the "stuff" he had. The fear Job had for God was not one which comes from freight or anxiety, instead it was a fear that was born out of reverential respect and worship for God, and Job proved that it had nothing to do with his 'blessings'.

The question for all of us to consider is, "was Job still 'blessed' after he lost everything: his wealth, health, marriage, children, and his reputation and status before his friends?" If your answer is a resounding "yes", then you agree that he being blessed was not based on what he possessed but rather based on what God spoke of him. Additionally, we can also infer that Job did not fear God because of the blessing (as the devil will have us believe), but rather he was blessed because he feared God, (**see Psalms 112**).

Hence instead of pursuing things like riches, a good marriage, good health and even pursuing God because of these things we consider being "the blessing", it will behoove us to have a paradigm shift in our thinking. We should begin to seek the ways in which we can truly position ourselves for the real "blessing", which is being "well spoken of" by God.

INTRODUCTION:

The best person who can really tell us what the blessing of God is; and also how to position ourselves to receive and walk in that blessing, is none other than the Lord Jesus Christ Himself. In one of His most profound and extensive sermons ever to be recorded; His main theme was announcing who the "blessed" person looked like, and what that person's blessedness procured for him or her in terms of their reward for having a certain specific attribute and attitude.

Sermon on the Mount:

The whole sermon, which is most affectionately referred to as "The Sermon on the Mount", is found in the Gospel of Mathew from Chapters Five through Seven. The attitudes or attributes which qualifies one as "blessed" is known in religious circles as the "Beatitudes", and they are contained in the first portion of the sermon in Chapter Five. In this one chapter alone, the Lord mentions the word "blessed" nine times and connects it each time to a specific reward any individual would receive as a result of having a particular attitude or attribute.

If the Lord or anyone for that matter stresses on a word like "blessed" nine times in one sermon, let alone in the first eleven verses of one Chapter of the Bible, that should really arouse our curiosity to discover everything there is to know about this word and ask for the grace, strength, and wisdom to walk in those attributes and attitudes that will cause us to receive the blessed reward or outcome.

Matthew 5:1-12: *"And seeing the multitudes, he went up into a mountain: and when he was set,* **his disciples came unto him***: And he opened his mouth, and taught them, saying,* **Blessed are the poor in spirit***: for theirs is the kingdom of heaven.* **Blessed are they that mourn***: for they shall be comforted.* **Blessed are the meek***: for they shall inherit the earth.* **Blessed are they which do hunger and thirst after righteousness***: for they shall be filled.* **Blessed are the merciful***: for they shall obtain mercy.* **Blessed are the pure in heart***: for they shall see God.* **Blessed are the peacemakers***: for they shall be called the children of God.* **Blessed are they which are persecuted for righteousness' sake***: for theirs is the kingdom of heaven.* **Blessed are ye***, when men shall revile you, and persecute you, and shall say all manner of evil against you falsely, for my sake. Rejoice, and be exceeding glad: for great is your reward in heaven: for so persecuted they the prophets which were before you"* (Emphasis mine)

Like many believers, I have casually glossed over the "Sermon on the Mount" many times over the years since my conversion and perhaps even before then as a religious Roman Catholic boy. However, a few years ago as I sought the Lord towards the beginning of the New Year, I felt compelled to read and study this sermon.

For the first time in my walk with the Lord, I sensed that something was about to alter the way I viewed my Christian walk. The Lord was putting a definite emphasis on "The Beatitudes" like He had never done in my life thus far.

As I read through, and casually studied the main themes with the help of a Bible Commentary, I realized that there was more to this sermon than I or anyone I knew then had embraced. For example, I took note for the first time that Matthew 5-7 were one and the same sermon by Jesus, and hence each of those chapters ought to be understood in context, and interpreted in concert with each other.

This new found interest in the sermon, obviously inspired by the Holy Spirit, caused me to search for more information on the subject since many of the concepts Jesus espoused did not make sense to me. One of the best resources I discovered was from Mike Bickle of the *International House of Prayer* in Kansas City, Missouri. His teaching on this subject and other

> THE "SERMON ON THE MOUNT" IS FOUNDATIONAL CHRISTIAN LIVING

subjects on prayer and intimacy with God have deeply enlightened and impacted my life, to say the least. He made me to appreciate even more what I believe the Holy Spirit was doing in me at the time. No longer was I going to gloss over this portion of scripture without consequence.

Christianity 101:

As Mike Bickle explains, this was not just another sermon Jesus was giving to His many followers, but rather to a few disciples. Jesus was actually expounding on what the "constitution" of His Kingdom is. He was declaring what the foundation of life in His Father's Kingdom should and would look like. Jesus was in effect giving His hearers who would hopefully become His disciples a course in what we may phrase, "Christianity 101".

Once again, this sermon has to be viewed by every believer in Jesus Christ as the basis and foundation of Christian living. It is with that in mind that Jesus at the end of His discourse describes two types of people who hear this sermon. The one who hears and does not walk accordingly; and the one who hears and builds his or her life on its principles accordingly:

Matthew 7:24-27: *"**Therefore whoever hears these sayings of Mine, and does them,** I will liken him to a wise man who built his house on the rock: and the rain descended, the floods came, and the winds blew and beat on that house; and it did not fall, for it was founded on the rock. But **everyone who hears these sayings of Mine, and does not do them,** will be like a foolish man who built his house on the sand: and the rain descended, the floods came, and the winds blew and beat on that house; and it fell. And great was its fall."* (Emphasis mine)

Even though it is good to apply this thought by Jesus of building your life on the "rock" of the whole Canon of scripture, (as many well do,) Jesus here is speaking specifically concerning the Kingdom principles He had just expounded in the previous two chapters. Those who adhere to and build their lives based on the principles outlined in "The Sermon on Mount," will be considered "blessed" or "wise" by God, and can withstand any adversity. However, those who choose to only gloss over or ignore the principles may seem to have some initial "success" in their life until adversity and the "storms" of life come crushing in.

A New Paradigm:

In the Sermon on the Mount, Jesus was also giving His hearers then and now a new standard of Kingdom thinking and living unlike what their manmade traditions and religious system had taught them for generations. However, this new paradigm was not necessarily "new" in terms of never having existed.

Even though it had always been the Father's way of thinking from the very beginning, it was new to the hearers because they were now hearing it for the first time directly from Him as the incarnate Jesus, and not from their flawed and insecure human leaders. Jesus made this distinction clear when He went back and forth between what their Rabbis or teachers had taught them, and what He was now revealing to them.

In Matthew 5:21-48, six different times Jesus stated: "You have heard that it was said by them of old time…**but I say to you…**" (*Paraphrase*)

Matthew 5:21-48: *"**You have heard that it was said to those of old,** "you shall not murder; and whoever murders will be in danger of the judgment: **But I say to you,** That whoever is angry with his brother without a cause shall be in danger of the judgment… **You have heard that it was said to those of old,** you shall not commit adultery: **But I say to you,** That whoever looks on a woman to lust for her has committed adultery with her already in his heart…"furthermore **It has been said,** Whoever divorces his wife, let him give her a certificate of divorce: **But I say to you,** That whoever divorces his wife, for any reason except sexual immorality, causes her to commit adultery… **Again, you have heard that it was said to those of old,** you shall not swear falsely, but shall perform your oaths to the Lord: **But I say to you,** do not swear at all; neither by heaven; for it is God's throne… **You have heard that it was said,** "An eye for an eye, and a tooth for a tooth" **But I tell you** not to resist an evil person: but whoever slaps you on your right cheek, turn the other to him also… **You have heard that it was said,** "You shall love your neighbor, and hate your enemy. **But I say to you,** Love your enemies, bless those who curse you, do good to those who hate you, and pray for those who spitefully use you, and persecute you…"* (Emphasis mine)

Without going into too much exposition, it is important to understand why Jesus was saying what it is He said in making a differentiation between what their leaders had informed them, and what He was NOW telling them. Jesus was not trying to give them a "new" instruction (as it were,) from what their spiritual fathers had handed down to them from generation to generation.

The different commandments Jesus was discussing were commandments contained in their "Torah" or "Pentateuch," (5 Books of Moses). Moses had received most of those commandments on Mount Sinai when he spoke with God face to face. However, after many generations and many interpretations which were mostly contained in their "Talmud," (Jewish Commentary), the true meaning and spirit of the commandments had been lost, and instead manmade traditions, enforced by the Pharisees and scribes were now in effect.

In fact, Jesus in another place chided these same leaders for making the law of God of no effect because of their manmade traditions, (**See Mark 7:5-13**). Therefore, when Jesus says to them, "but I say unto you…", He is revealing His pre-incarnate knowledge of what God meant when He first gave the commandments; because after all, He was there with the Father on Mount Sinai when He spoke to Moses. No wonder that the initial response of the crowd after Jesus was done speaking was that of amazement, not only because of what was said, but more importantly the authority with which He spoke:

Matthew 7:28-29: *"And it came to pass, when Jesus had ended these sayings, the people were astonished at his* *doctrine: **For he taught them as one having authority,** and not as the scribes"* (Emphasis mine)

As I have continued to seek the Lord concerning what it means to live the Kingdom lifestyle from the "Sermon on the Mount" perspective, He has graciously revealed to me some of His unsearchable riches on this subject through illumination in His Word, and also allowed me to personally experience certain situations in my life that required me to respond with a "Sermon on the Mount" mindset or attitude. I have done well in certain areas, and not so well in others. I am on a journey or quest to discover everything God has in store for me in the deep recesses of His Heart. I am on a mission to encounter Him in order that I might reveal Him to others. Jesus made it clear that the way to be truly "blessed" is by reading, understanding, living, and teaching "The Sermon on the Mount" lifestyle.

I believe with all my heart that we will all be judged at the end of this age more on our attitude and response towards this sermon by Jesus, than by any great or small "accomplishment" we may have achieved in ministry or in the market place. In fact, Jesus confirms this when he actually connects greatness in God's Kingdom with how well we have walked out the principles in the "Sermon on the Mount":

Matthew 5:19: *"Whosoever therefore shall break one of **these least commandments,** and shall teach men so, **he shall be called the least** in the kingdom of heaven: but whosoever **shall do and teach them,** the same **shall be***

called great in the kingdom of heaven" (Emphasis mine)

I have decided, through the conviction of the Holy Spirit, to begin each year by contemplating the significance of this Sermon in my life, and also judge myself on how far I have come in incorporating the attitudes or attributes espoused by Jesus in Matthew 5-7. I also check myself concerning which attributes or areas in my life that I am still lacking.

I pray this is your pursuit also; otherwise I would be surprised you have gotten this far reading this book. If not, however, seek the Lord diligently as you continue to read, in addition to other resources on the subject and I know God will reveal its importance in your life like He so graciously did me. *(Mike Bickle's teaching on the "Sermon on the Mount" lifestyle is a great resource I would definitely recommend. You can get it on his website at www.mikebickle.org)*

How Can This Be?

Before delving into the details of the subject, it is important to state that the requirements for the "Sermon on the Mount" lifestyle are not easy to fulfill if approached by our own wisdom and strength. I believe it is the reason that many in the Church ignore its tenets, because it seems so difficult, impossible, and utterly impractical to live by these standards. However, before you give up know that there is hope!

One of the greatest revelations in the Word of God you can ever receive is that there is nothing God ever asks of you and me to be and do that He is not already done or is doing Himself. In addition, whenever He tells you and me to be or do something, He already knows we are incapable in our own strength to be it or do it. He is not looking at us to work out something He has not already worked into our hearts. What He is looking for from us is first and foremost, a heart that

> THERE IS NOTHING GOD ASKS YOU TO DO THAT HE HIMSELF HAS NOT ALREADY DONE

says, "Yes Lord! If you want me to be this or do that, I agree with you; and by your grace, strength, and leadership I will be this and do that." In other words, He is first looking for agreement from us, as weak and incomplete as our agreement may be. The Apostle Paul puts it this way, *"For if there be first a willing mind, it is accepted ..." (2 Cor. 8:12)*.

Paul once upon a time also stated one of the most quoted verses of scripture about how we ought to *"...work out [our] own salvation with fear and trembling"* (**Phil. 2:12**). However the reason why many say it, but few seem to be able to really "work out" their salvation is because we have not stressed verse 13 enough as the basis for which we are able to accomplish verse 12:

Philippians 2:13: *"for it is God who **works in you** both to will and to do for His good pleasure"* (Emphasis mine)

Again let me admonish you even as I admonish myself to stop trying to "work out" what we have not first sought God to "work in". It is not by your will power or intellectual strength that will make you successful in living "The Sermon on the Mount" lifestyle which is God's ultimate "good pleasure" for you and me. That is why Jesus made prayer and fasting two of the main cornerstones upon which this lifestyle of blessedness can be fully accomplished. We will explore these cornerstones plus another in the final chapter of this book, and discover how they relate with achieving the "blessed" life Jesus has in-store for us.

Becoming Like Him:

As stated earlier, when Jesus gives us an instruction concerning becoming or doing something, He has already done or is doing it. He is the ultimate Leader who leads us by example.

For example, When God tells you and me to love or give; He has already loved and given the ultimate gift. Hence the goal of "The Sermon on the Mount" lifestyle is to be like the Trinity. Jesus expressly made that the goal and apex of the believer when He said at the end of Matthew 5:

Matthew 5:48: *"Therefore you shall be perfect, just as your Father in heaven is perfect"*

It is noteworthy that all the attributes and attitudes prescribed by Jesus in His Sermon are attributes and attitudes that He Himself as fully Man and fully God expressed in His life while on earth, and even now at the right Hand of the Father in Heaven. And of course, we know that the Blessed Holy Spirit is no different than the Father or the Son, but on the contrary is the One through whom we are even able to get a glimpse of the God Head as He reveals and manifests their nature and attributes to us and through us.

Don't Sell Yourself Short:

Some people, maybe including you my reader, might still be unconvinced about the possibility of really living this lifestyle. They readily give the age old excuse many in the Church have employed for generations by saying, "it was easy for Jesus to live the way He did and do the things He did because after all He is God. Hence, we mere fallen mortals should not be expected to live like Jesus or do the things He did".

Even though the reason "why" and "how" Jesus lived and did what He did has been debated by theologians for years, the lame excuse and argument that we are incapable of being like Him or doing what He did falls flat in the light of scripture. As believers in the Lord Jesus, we have a choice to make: we are either going to believe what Jesus said or we are not.

When Jesus told His Disciples that if they believed on Him, they would do the works He had done, and even greater works would they do; I don't read anywhere that Peter (their favorite Spokesman) raised his hand to object to what Jesus had just told them because He was God and they were not. Thank God they believed and received what their Master told them at face value, and true to His Word, the Book of Acts recounts all the works and greater works those fallen, mere mortals, filled with the same Power of the Holy Spirit Jesus was filled with did to reach their then known world with the character and Gospel of the Lord Jesus Christ within hundred years.

If Jesus said it, then don't sell yourself short; but rise up with boldness and say "Lord if you say this is my portion, then I want it".

Remember that He will help and equip you with grace, strength, and wisdom to walk it out; but you have to want it, ask for it, and be willing to trust His leadership. If you fall or fail (which you most definitely will), rise up, repent, and keep on moving forward in Him. For with every step you take (moving forward) and with every turn your heart is moved toward Him, there is a God who is smiling and "speaking well" of you.

A Man after His Own Heart:

Recently, as I have continued to meditate on "the Sermon on the Mount", the Lord revealed the most incredible thing to me which then became the final inspiration to write this book. As much as it should suffice that we follow Jesus' example of living this lifestyle of blessedness, the Lord understands our hesitation because of what many leaders; many of whom sincerely do not know any better, have said about our inability to become like Jesus or live like He did due to His deity and our lack thereof.

The Lord, therefore, revealed to me a *man* who lived this lifestyle. He is considered by many, including myself, as their most favorite bible character; and whose life many say they want to emulate. This was a man who was brought from absolute obscurity to prominence and became the ruler of his people. This was a fearless warrior who brought down giants and caused his enemies hearts to fail them; and yet had the tenderest heart of worship and intimacy toward God than anyone before him, and perhaps anyone after him.

This was the man who received what I consider to be the greatest compliment any created being could receive, no less, coming from the very lips of the Majesty on High. Many in scripture have received worthy commendation from God for their love, devotion, and dedication to Him, but to no one has scripture recorded this:

Acts 13:22: *"... He raised up for them **David as king**, to whom also He gave testimony and said, 'I have found David the son of Jesse, **a man after My own heart**, **who will do all My will'"** (Emphasis mine)

In the proceeding chapters of this book, we will explore the characteristics of the life of David as related to "the

Sermon on the Mount" lifestyle that Jesus admonishes all His disciples to adhere to in order to be considered "blessed".

King David pursued this lifestyle in the Old Covenant, without the indwelling and enabling power and presence of the Holy Ghost which we so graciously possess in the New Covenant. The writer of Hebrews makes it clear that we who are living under the New Covenant have a better covenant than those under the Old covenant based on better promises made by the Father to His Son:

Heb. 8:6: *"But now He has obtained a more excellent ministry, inasmuch as He is also Mediator of a better covenant, which was established on better promises"*

Heb. 12:24: *"to Jesus the Mediator of the new covenant, and to the blood of sprinkling that speaks better things than that of Abel"*

If David was "well spoken of" by God because he made as his obsession and passion to live by the principles outlined by Jesus in His Sermon on the Mount thousands of years before Jesus even showed up, we have no more excuse not to give due diligence to this Sermon, and position our hearts to receive grace and strength to walk thereby. Jesus said we will be blessed if we do it.

Do you sincerely endeavor to live and enjoy the Kingdom lifestyle? Do you want to have a heart ablaze with passion for God's presence? Do you want to be considered great in the eyes of God as you walk according to the beatitudes? Do you want to have an impact in this world, and in the one to come? If your answer is "Yes" then come with me as we explore the attitudes and rewards of the "Sermon on the Mount" lifestyle.

There are eight blessings the Lord wants to release into your life, but there are eight corresponding attitudes you must have in order to receive these blessings. Let us take a look at each one of these attitudes and corresponding blessings, and discover how Jesus and King David applied it to their own lives and therefore are considered BLESSED.

Chapter 1

POOR IN SPIRIT: *Passion for His Presence*

Blessed are the poor in spirit: for theirs is the kingdom of heaven (Matthew 5:3).

ONE of the most intriguing aspects of the "Sermon on the Mount" is the seeming contradiction in the beatitudes that qualify us to be blessed. For example Jesus begins His great sermon with "Blessed are the poor in spirit..." That obviously must have gotten everyone's attention, because we do not usually associate blessedness with poverty.

It is helpful that Jesus qualified what kind of poverty He was referring to. It was not poverty in material things, but poverty of spiritual things. Jesus is saying that the Kingdom of God belongs to those who recognize their impoverishment when it comes to spiritual things. What does it mean to be "poor in spirit"?

Being "poor in spirit" is to acknowledge our utter dependence on God's grace and help to sustain our wholeheartedness in Him. It is a call to humility in dealing with our human condition, in relation with God's standards. In other words, the ones who are "poor in spirit" are the ones who are humble enough to acknowledge the depth of their need of God. They recognize that their life is void without God's intervening love and presence. They have emptied their hearts of worldly mindsets, and are actively positioning their hearts before the Lord to be enriched by Him.

Although some may want to apply this attribute mostly to those who may be considered "poor" by worldly standards, this has nothing to do with having material or physical possessions or not. In fact, as we will soon see, David was one of the richest men in all of history, and yet on more than a few occasions acknowledged his "poverty" of soul and spirit.

There are poor people in material possessions that are not "poor in spirit". That means, even though they lack material wealth, their hearts are filled up with pride and worldly and ungodly mindsets; and hence do not acknowledge the need or poverty of their spirit and soul. However, there are people who are rich by worldly standards, having lots of possessions, who acknowledge the utter poverty of their spirit and soul which can only be enriched and satisfied by God.

In Isaiah 66:2, God describes the kind of person He is attracted to and who will receive an audience from Him:

Isaiah 66:2: *"For all those things My hand has made, And all those things exist," Says the LORD. "But **on this one will I look**: On him who is **poor** and of a **contrite spirit**, And who trembles at My word"* (Emphasis mine)

In other words, God makes it perfectly clear the type of attitude of heart He expects those who will approach Him to have. He is looking for the one who has a humble and smitten or repentant spirit or heart. One who is not "full of him or herself", and hence does not actively acknowledge their dependence on Him. In fact, He says through James the Pastor that he actively will oppose and resist the proud, but release more grace to the person who has a poor or humble spirit or heart:

James 4:6: *"But He gives more grace. Therefore He says: "God resists the proud, but gives grace to the humble"*

Jesus described this difference when he gave the parable of the two men who went up to the Temple to pray. The one was a Pharisee and the other a publican or sinner. Among these two men, the one who actually received audience with God was the Publican because he was the one who was "poor in spirit".

Luke 18:9-14: *"Also He spoke this parable to some who trusted in themselves that they were righteous, and despised others: "Two men went up to the temple to pray, one a Pharisee and the other a tax collector. The*

Pharisee stood and prayed thus with himself, 'God, I thank You that I am not like other men—extortioners, unjust, adulterers, or even as this tax collector. I fast twice a week; I give tithes of all that I possess.' And the tax collector, standing afar off, would not so much as raise his eyes to heaven, but beat his breast, saying, 'God, be merciful to me a sinner!' I tell you, this man went down to his house justified rather than the other; for everyone who exalts himself will be humbled, and he who humbles himself will be exalted"

This beatitude, being poor in spirit, is so important and foundational. It is the first attribute Jesus referenced when describing who He had been anointed and sent to proclaim the Gospel of the Kingdom. In His first public sermon, Jesus made it clear He had been sent to those who were poor in spirit:

Luke 4:18: *"The Spirit of the Lord is upon me, because He has anointed me to preach the gospel to the poor; He has sent me to heal the brokenhearted, to proclaim liberty to the captives and recovery of sight to the blind, to set at liberty those who are oppressed"*

I have heard quite a lot of preachers, especially some who overemphasize the "Prosperity Gospel", use this scripture to prove that Jesus came to deliver us from physical poverty. In other words, He came to preach the gospel so the poor will be poor no more. In as much as I agree to some extent that this scripture can apply to that supposition, I believe it is not the main idea Jesus was projecting to His listeners that day.

Jesus was not primarily referring to the materially poor, but the spiritually poor. In other words He was saying His anointing, mission, and assignment was to those who recognized their spiritual bankruptcy in relation to their relationship with a Holy God. These also recognize their utter dependence on His

> JESUS' MISSION IS TO THOSE WHO RECOGNIZE THEIR SPIRITUAL BANKRUPTCY

mercy and grace to restore them to full fellowship with Him. To such, He offered the good news of the Kingdom of God.

This was not, however, the condition of most of His hearers that day. These were the religious elites who considered themselves already rich, full, and qualified for God's benevolence.

Jesus confirmed this in another place, when He used another metaphor to describe to whom His ministry, assignment, and blessing was to: He came as a physician to help those who recognized they were sick.

Mark 2:16 – 17: *"And when the scribes and Pharisees saw Him eating with the tax collectors and sinners, they said to His disciples, "How is it that He eats and drinks with tax collectors and sinners?" When Jesus heard it, He said to them, **"Those who are well have no need of a physician, but those who are sick. I did not come to call the righteous, but sinners, to repentance"***
(Emphasis mine)

5

When we act as though we have no need of a vibrant relationship with God at a heart level; when we feel like we have "arrived", especially in ministry, due to our seeming success because of our notoriety and material blessing; when we take for granted His love and grace, without pursuing wholehearted obedience to God, we fall into the same predicament of the religious leaders in Jesus' day. Worse of all, we portray the same image of the Laodicean church described in the Book of Revelation.

I humbly submit that the Body of Christ in many parts of the world, especially in the Western hemisphere, has become just like the Church in Laodicea who Jesus said made God sick to the stomach, that He has to spew them out.

Revelation 3:14 – 20: *""And to the angel of the church of the Laodiceans write, 'These things says the Amen, the Faithful and True Witness, the Beginning of the creation of God: "I know your works, that you are neither cold nor hot. I could wish you were cold or hot. So then, because you are lukewarm, and neither cold nor hot, I will vomit you out of My mouth.* **Because you say, 'I am rich, have become wealthy, and have need of nothing'**—*and do not know that you are wretched, miserable, poor, blind, and naked— I counsel you to buy from Me gold refined in the fire, that you may be rich; and white garments, that you may be clothed, that the shame of your nakedness may not be revealed; and anoint your eyes with eye salve, that you may see. As many as I love, I rebuke and chasten. Therefore be zealous and repent. Behold, I stand at the door and*

6

knock. If anyone hears My voice and opens the door, I will come in to him and dine with him, and he with Me" " (Emphasis mine)

The attitude of the Laodicean church is so much akin to our current state in the Body of Christ. Their lackadaisical attitude in pursuing the presence of God was so obvious that it made God "sick to His stomach". This attitude was as a result of their apparent lack of a poverty of spirit since they assumed God was pleased with their apparent "success".

They had everything going for them in ministry: they had the latest marketing techniques; the latest technology and the best musicians and preachers, (teachers) who told them exactly what they wanted to hear. Their offering plates never ran dry and building projects were always well funded. They had everything but God Himself!

While some of the other churches mentioned before they endured hardship and persecution because of their faith, this church lived and thrived in relative ease and comfort. They knew how to put on a show, but in spite of all this, Jesus said that His presence was not in their midst. They had become proud; drunken and blinded by their own "success", and needed to repent.

I have asked myself many times how is it possible to have a "party" for someone while the person stands outside the door, wanting desperately to come in. That's exactly what Jesus told the church then and now in verse

20. He desperately wanted to have intimacy and fellowship with them, but they were not desperately acknowledging their need for Him. He desired to cover their nakedness and give them a fresh revelation of Himself.

Jesus does not mind our material riches. In fact He is delighted to give you and me more. However, He minds when we are not actively acknowledging our poverty of spirit, and actively pursuing Him to fill our poverty stricken souls with the richness of His love, presence, and power. We need to rid ourselves in this generation of the Laodicean spirit, and embrace an active pursuit of God and His presence in our lives and in our churches.

David's Passion for His Presence:

As we have mentioned earlier, David received the greatest compliment of all when God spoke concerning him that "he was a man after God's own Heart". This 'eulogy' from God did not come lightly. David was a man who decided from his youth that he would position his heart before God as well as seek Him early and often until he knew what moved His heart.

When the Prophet Samuel arrived at Jesse's door step to find and anoint the next king of Israel, (after the rejection of Saul by God,) he was presented with seven sons that seemed more qualified and dignified than David who was not even invited to the 'anointing service'. However, each time the Prophet concluded he had made the right choice based on the outward appearance of the son, God stopped him in his tracks. God that day revealed to His beloved prophet that His criteria of giving His Kingdom was not based on any external attribute or appearance, but based solely on the attitude and position of the heart of the candidate.

1 Samuel 16:7: *"But the LORD said to Samuel, 'Do not look at his appearance or at his physical stature, because I have refused him. For the LORD does not see as man sees; for man looks at the outward appearance, but the LORD looks at the heart.'"*

And so it was that after all seven sons passed before Samuel that David was brought from the backside of the wilderness, where he attended to the sheep of his father, and was anointed before his 'more qualified' brothers to be King of Israel. God thus revealed to us that He would rather we seek to have a heart that is positioned in humility before Him, rather than an outward appearance of strength and self dependence. His Word still declares:

Romans 9:16: *"So then it is not of him who wills, nor of him who runs, but of God who shows mercy"*

Zechariah 4:6: *"So he answered and said to me: "This is the word of the LORD to Zerubbabel: 'Not by might nor by power, but by My Spirit,' Says the LORD of hosts"*

What was so special about David was that throughout his life, especially during his reign as king, he recognized that he was nothing except God's mercy and power was extended towards him. David always acknowledged his utter dependence on God, which is reflected over and over in the Psalms which he wrote. He often expressed the poverty of his soul, even though he had everything this world had to offer: wealth, fame, beautiful women, honor, influence; you name it he had it. Yet, none of these privileges could ever replace the void and ache of his heart and soul for the presence of God. He may have been rich in the physical sense, but he was a man who was "poor in spirit".

> DAVID WOULD RATHER LOSE HIS KINGDOM THAN ALLOW HIS SOUL TO LOSE ITS PURSUIT OF GOD'S PRESENCE

This knowledge drove him to seek God more than anyone in his kingdom, including the poor in the society. David would rather give up his earthly kingdom with all its perks, than allow his soul to become complacent and lose its pursuit of God and His Presence.

Unlike Saul, David's heart was so smitten and contrite when he was confronted about his sin of adultery and murder; he threw himself before God (not the Prophet) and confessed his sin. In his confession, which is recorded in Psalms 51, he made it clear what was more important to him... the Presence of God.

Psalm 51:10-11: *"Create in me a clean heart, O God, And renew a steadfast spirit within me. Do not cast me away from Your presence, And do not take Your Holy Spirit from me"*

David was not concerned about the fact that he could lose the kingdom, like Saul did, because of his sin which in the eyes of some was worse than Saul's. His major concern was that he might lose the Presence of God. In other words, David was crying to God and saying, "if you decide to take away the kingdom and all its benefits, I will be alright; but please don't take your Spirit and Presence from me, for then I will be totally undone!" As a result of this posture, God preserved David and his kingdom even though he was chastised.

> SAUL WAS MORE CONCERNED WITH HIS REPUTATION THAN THE INTEGRITY AND POVERTY OF HIS SPIRIT

That is the exact opposite approach King Saul took when he was confronted with his disobedience, (**1 Sam. 15**). First of all, he tried to rationalize his sin before the Prophet Samuel and then when that failed he implored Samuel to still honor him before the people. Saul was more concerned about his reputation and status before the people and not the integrity and poverty of his heart or spirit before the God who appointed him to be King. No wonder God rejected King Saul and actually removed His Presence from his life.

A few more of the scriptures that highlight David as a man who was "poor in spirit" are as follows:

Psalms 34:6: *"This poor man cried out, and the LORD heard him, And saved him out of all his troubles"*

Psalms 40:17: *"But I am poor and needy; Yet the LORD thinks upon me. You are my help and my deliverer; Do not delay, O my God"*

Psalms 69:29: *"But I am poor and sorrowful; Let Your salvation, O God, set me up on high"*

What is particularly interesting about these scriptures is that they are applicable to the Lord Jesus, and are known as the Messianic Psalms. Even though they were prayers that David prayed because of his circumstances, he was invariably prophesying about the life and work of the Lord Jesus who would also go through similar circumstances. One of Jesus' names or titles is "the son of David". This title refers more to the fact that Jesus would exhibit many of the characteristics of David's life, than the fact that He was a direct descendant of David. The writers of the Gospels recognized this fact and they were certain to make sure that they made a note whenever Jesus fulfilled any of David's Psalms. One of the most common ones is Psalm 69.

Psalms 69:9: *"Because zeal for Your house has eaten me up, And the reproaches of those who reproach You have fallen on me"*

The Apostle John noted this fulfillment after Jesus had gone into the Temple and overturned the tables of the money changers, when he wrote:

John 2:17: *"Then His disciples remembered that it was written, "zeal for your house has eaten me up""*

Kingdom Blessing:

According to Jesus, the "blessedness" associated with being "poor in spirit" is that you will receive "the Kingdom of God". In other words, the Kingdom of God is the reward that one receives as a result of exhibiting the attitude and attributes of humility and poverty of spirit. Conversely, it also implies that no one can receive the Kingdom of God without this important trait. Does it mean that one can be saved and yet miss out on the blessing of the kingdom of God?

To answer such an important question, it is necessary for us to define what the 'Kingdom of God' is. Often, many are quick to confuse "Heaven" as being the same as the "Kingdom of God". Although Heaven is part of the Kingdom of God, it is not the Kingdom of God Jesus was referring to. Heaven is the celestial geographical place where God's throne currently is located, while the "Kingdom of God" is every realm and sphere that God's rule and dominion is acknowledged, manifested and enforced.

In other words, the Kingdom of God is not limited to just a geographical place like Heaven. Rather it can be explained as what happens in a life or any region when the influence of God's dominion, with all that He is and has, is acknowledged in that life or region. The Kingdom is therefore a mindset which influences the lifestyle of those who possess it.

> THE KINGDOM OF GOD IS A MINDSET WHICH INFLUENCES YOUR LIFESTYLE

This is the reason why both John the Baptist and Jesus began their public ministry preaching the same thing. They both spoke of the need for the people to have a new mindset, for the advent of a new kingdom was upon them:

Matthew 3:1 – 2: *"In those days John the Baptist came preaching in the wilderness of Judea, and saying, "Repent, for the kingdom of heaven is at hand!""*

Matthew 4:17: *"From that time Jesus began to preach and to say, "Repent, for the kingdom of heaven is at hand""*

To repent simply means to have a change of mind and perspective or as Strong's Dictionary puts it, "to think differently"₂. Jesus and John (The Baptist) both prescribed a new way of seeing and doing things in this new "Kingdom of God", unlike how things were done with respect to the kingdom their listeners were now a part of, which was epitomized by the Roman Empire at the time.

There are more references in scripture about the "Kingdom of God" or "Kingdom of Heaven" than "Church" or just "Heaven". My point is, for so long we have preached more to people about how they can make it to Heaven by getting saved and going to Church, than actually relaying the Kingdom of God lifestyle that is required now, and also will be made fully manifest when Jesus sets up His eternal Kingdom on Earth in His Second

GOD IS PASSIONATE IN EXPOSING AND IMPOSING HIS KINGDOM ON EARTH THROUGH YOU

Coming. Don't misunderstand me; going to Heaven when we die is a vital perspective for us to keep and preach, but there is more God has in store for the believer here on Earth, now, and in the hereafter. God is more passionate and interested in exposing Himself and imposing His Kingdom on Earth through you and me than we could ever imagine.

More than any other subject, the Kingdom is the one thing Jesus focused on in His preaching and in His lesson on prayer to His Disciples. The phrase "Kingdom of God" (not counting Kingdom of Heaven) appears 231 times in the Gospels alone, even though most of the occurrences are duplicated from one Gospel to the next. Never-the-less, it shows how emphatic Jesus was on the concept or subject of the "Kingdom" that His disciples never forgot its preeminence in their recounting of Jesus' life and ministry. It was that important that when Jesus sent out His Disciples to go preach, that was the message they were to deliver:

15

Luke 9:2: *"He sent them to preach the kingdom of God and to heal the sick"*

When it also came time for Him to teach His disciples how to pray, one of the important requests Jesus taught them to demand from God was, "...Your kingdom come":

Luke 11:2: *"So He said to them, "When you pray, say: Our Father in heaven, Hallowed be Your name. **Your kingdom come**. Your will be done On earth as it is in heaven"* (Emphasis mine)

What Is The Kingdom of God?

The Apostle Paul gave us one of the clearest insights into what the Kingdom of God is when He wrote to the Church at Rome:

Rom. 14:17: *"for the kingdom of God is not eating and drinking, but righteousness and peace and joy in the Holy Spirit"*

In essence, the three ingredients that characterize any one or any place that claims to have the Kingdom of God will be righteousness, peace, and joy in the presence of the Holy Ghost. Therefore, it will be perfectly within the context of what Jesus meant in the Sermon on the Mount to render Matt. 5:3 as: *"Well spoken of by God are the poor in spirit, for theirs is the righteousness, peace, and joy in the Holy Ghost"* (paraphrase).

Another way to perceive the "Kingdom of God" is that it represents the economy of God. This means that it represents everything that God is and has. It entails, but is not limited to, His power, provision, protection, promotion, direction, and so on and so forth.

The Apostle Peter helps us understand that the born again child of God has the unique opportunity and privilege to be a partaker of God's nature:

2 Peter 1:3 – 4: *"as His divine power has given to us all things that pertain to life and godliness, through the knowledge of Him who called us by glory and virtue, by which have been given to us exceedingly great and precious promises, that through these **you may be partakers of the divine nature**, having escaped the corruption that is in the world through lust"* (Emphasis mine)

God's Divine nature has everything to do with who He is, which is then available to all those who are in His Kingdom or realm of His influence. His Divine nature of holiness, health, wealth, wisdom, and glory is therefore available to be imparted to those who are "poor in spirit".

In fact, every attribute we see in Jesus, we have claim to if we adhere to the principles laid out by Jesus in the Sermon on the Mount. Since we are "Joint Heirs" with Jesus, what is spoken about Jesus in the Book of Revelation can be ours in measure now and even more so in the Resurrection. These seven attributes of "The Lamb" can be yours and mine if we follow Him diligently:

Revelation 5:12: *"saying with a loud voice: "Worthy is the Lamb who was slain To receive **power** and **riches** and **wisdom**, And **strength** and **honor** and **glory** and **blessing!"** "* (Emphasis mine)

So why don't you make it a priority in your life to be "poor spirit". A passion for His presence will grant you access into His treasury of goodness we have not yet experienced.

Chapter 2

MOURNING: *The Intercessor's Heart*

Blessed are they that mourn: for they shall be comforted
(Matthew 5:4)

THE second attribute Jesus mentions in His discourse on the Mount which attracts God's favor is "mourning". Just like the first, this beatitude seems to have a negative connotation. Mourning is mostly associated with grief or sorrow. As much as this term seems to be a negative attitude, and as much as we would rather like to avoid it since it suggests a loss of something or someone precious; it is also an attitude God would love to see in us especially when it relates to our attitude towards our sin and that of others around us.

First, we have been told to have a "poor spirit" which means to acknowledge our own poverty of godliness before a Holy and Righteous God. Jesus now proceeds to show us how our attitude should be when we see the chasm between us and God. In other words, when I acknowledge my own weaknesses and sinfulness before God, having the privilege to see His Holiness, my only response will be to mourn or grieve over the gap that I see between Him and myself.

The Apostle Paul encouraged the Corinthian Church to restore the brother who was having an adulterous affair with his father's wife because he did not only acknowledge that what he was doing was wrong, but he also showed remorse or sorrow over the sin. In other words, he mourned over his sin. Without a true attitude of mourning over our sins, there cannot also be a true attitude of repentance; because as Paul stated to the church it is godly sorrow or mourning that leads us to repentance.

2 Corinthians 7:9 – 11: *"Now I rejoice, not that you were made sorry, but that **your sorrow led to repentance**. For you were made sorry in a godly manner, that you might suffer loss from us in nothing. **For godly sorrow produces repentance** leading **to salvation**, not to be regretted; but the sorrow of the world produces death. For observe this very thing, that you sorrowed in a godly manner: What diligence it produced in you, what clearing of yourselves, what indignation, what fear, what vehement desire, what zeal, what vindication! In all things you proved yourselves to be clear in this matter"* (Emphasis mine)

It seems that it is impossible to have godly sorrow without first an acknowledgement of the vast separation between our sinful nature and God's absolute holiness and purity. This means that the prerequisite for having godly sorrow or a mournful attitude over your sin is first having a poverty of spirit as discussed in the previous chapter.

I have found this to be the case in my own experience that as long as I compared myself with those around me who lived an obviously sinful life, I never felt the compulsion to mourn over my own sin. When we have a horizontal view and attitude towards the sins of others in comparison to our own perceived righteousness, like the Pharisees of Jesus' day, we are devoid of a poverty of spirit and hence cannot mourn over our own sin.

> WITHOUT A TRUE ATTITUDE OF MOURNING OVER SIN, THERE CANNOT BE TRUE REPENTANCE

However, when we become poor in spirit and are confronted with a vertical view of the Holy One who sits in judgment over all, we are suddenly struck with utter shame at our own filthiness in comparison with His absolute holiness and purity.

Woe Is Me!

This was the experience of Isaiah the Prophet when He encountered the Glory of God in the Temple. If you subscribe to the chronological arrangement of the Book of Isaiah as I do, you will agree that it is obvious that Isaiah had been operating in the office of the Prophet up until his encounter in Isaiah Chapter 6 after the mighty King Uzziah died.

Isaiah 6:1 – 4: *"In the year that King Uzziah died, I saw the Lord sitting on a throne, high and lifted up, and the train of His robe filled the temple. Above it stood seraphim; each one had six wings: with two he covered his face, with two he covered his feet, and with two he flew. And one cried to another and said: "Holy, holy, holy is the LORD of hosts; The whole earth is full of His glory!" And the posts of the door were shaken by the voice of him who cried out, and the house was filled with smoke"*

A little background to this episode in Isaiah's life would help us better understand the Prophet's attitude up until this encounter. The reign of King Uzziah, who was king of Israel at this time, had been quite a success. It was during a time of military success, national prosperity and pride. However, in the midst of all the success, the nation was also in spiritual decline (sounds familiar?). Although King Uzziah had been sequestered from the public view, due to the leprosy which he was stricken with when he attempted to burn incense before the Lord over the objections of the Priests, he was still famous among his people. His former pride and punishment as a result of his presumption were not deterrents in him still being regarded in high esteem by the people, including the prophet who, by the way, was of royal blood.

For many years, the Prophet Isaiah, who considered himself to be righteous, took the liberty to remind and scold the nation of Israel of their sin, and hence God's imminent judgment upon them if they did not repent. We see this played out in Chapters one to five of Isaiah. Especially in Chapter five, he goes into a series of "woes" against those that perpetrate certain evils. Unbeknown to him, he was about to woe himself when He saw the Glory of God.

Isaiah 6: 5 – 7: *"So I said: "**Woe is me, for I am undone!** **Because I am a man of unclean lips,** And I dwell in the midst of a people of unclean lips; For my eyes have seen the King, The LORD of hosts." Then one of the seraphim flew to me, having in his hand a live coal which he had taken with the tongs from the altar. And he touched my mouth with it, and said: "Behold, this has touched your lips; Your iniquity is taken away, And your sin purged.""* (Emphasis mine)

On this day, Isaiah came face to face with his own sinfulness and had to cry out to God for help. When he finally discovered the chasm between God's holiness and his own folly, a spiritual grief or sorrow overcame him. When he cried out in his grief, God released one of the angels to purge him of his uncleanness with a hot coal. When we are convicted of our sins, do we ignore the dealings of the Spirit of God by rationalizing our sins; or do we become truly remorseful and seek God's help in repentance?

David, a Man of Sorrow:

King David is another perfect example of someone who understood how to mourn or have godly sorrow over his sin and shortcomings. Time after time when he fell short of God's expectations for him, he refused to rationalize his actions or decisions even though as the King it would have been easy for him to do so.

As was mentioned earlier in the previous Chapter, one of the reasons why God rejected King Saul was his inability to take responsibility for his own shortcomings and have godly sorrow over his sins. When he was confronted by the Prophet Samuel about his disobedience concerning not utterly destroying the Amelikites, he initially denied the charge, then rationalized his decision to spare the King and some of the animals. When his rationalizing fell short, he still would not be remorseful and seek God's pardon, but rather asked the Prophet to uphold his reputation before the people.

1 Samuel 15:19 – 30: *"Why then did you not obey the voice of the LORD? ... And Saul said to Samuel, "**But I have obeyed the voice of the LORD, and gone on the mission on which the LORD sent me, and brought back Agag king of Amalek;** I have utterly destroyed the Amalekites... Then Saul said to Samuel, "I have sinned, for I have transgressed the commandment of the LORD and your words, **because I feared the people and obeyed their voice.** Now therefore, please pardon my sin, and return with me, that I may worship the LORD." But Samuel said to Saul, "I will not return with you, for* *you have rejected the word of the LORD, and the LORD has rejected you from being king over Israel."..." Then he said, "I have sinned; yet **honor me now, please, before the elders of my people and before Israel**, and return with me, that I may worship the LORD your God""* (Emphasis mine)

However, King David had a totally different attitude when he was confronted by another prophet about his adulterous affair with Bathsheba, and the murder of her husband. He immediately broke down before God, not the Prophet, and mourned over his obvious indiscretion and pleaded for forgiveness and mercy.

2 Samuel 12:13: *"So David said to Nathan, "I have sinned against the LORD." And Nathan said to David, "The LORD also has put away your sin; you shall not die"*

One of the famous Psalms in the bible is an actual prayer David prayed during this period of mourning and repenting. It gives you and me an insight into the heart of this King and what was more important to him than a kingdom.

Psalm 51:1 – 19: *"...Have mercy upon me, O God, According to Your lovingkindness; ... Blot out my transgressions. Wash me thoroughly from my iniquity, And cleanse me from my sin. For **I acknowledge my transgressions**, And my sin is always before me. **Against You, You only, have I sinned**... Hide Your face from my sins, And blot out all my iniquities. Create*

25

in me a clean heart, O God, And renew a steadfast spirit within me. **Do not cast me away from Your presence, And do not take Your Holy Spirit from me.** *Restore to me the joy of Your salvation, And uphold me by Your generous Spirit...* **The sacrifices of God are a broken spirit, A broken and a contrite heart—** *These, O God, You will not despise..."* (Emphasis mine)

The Intercessor's Heart:

Even though it is important to learn how to mourn over our own short comings especially in the light of God's revelation of Himself to us; it is equally important to also learn how to mourn over the sins of our nations, cities, and neighborhoods. In fact, God expects us to mourn because it forms one of the most basic aspects of true intercession.

In one of the most revealing passages in the bible, God revealed to His Prophet Ezekiel His intentions for the city of Jerusalem because of the abominations being committed in it. However only those who were mourning over the city's sins would be spared from the imminent judgment.

Ezekiel 9:4 – 6: *"and the LORD said to him, "Go through the midst of the city, through the midst of Jerusalem, and* **put a mark on the foreheads of the men who sigh and cry over all the abominations that are done within it."** *To the others He said in my hearing, "Go after him through the city and kill; do not let your eye spare, nor have any pity. Utterly slay old and young men, maidens* *and little children and women; **but do not come near anyone on whom** is **the mark;** and begin at My sanctuary."* So they began with the elders who were before the temple"* (Emphasis mine)

Throughout biblical history, we witness some of the great patriarchs of the faith assume this attitude of mourning and subsequent intercession in relation to the sin and devastation of their nation, or impending judgment. From Jeremiah, Nehemiah, Daniel, Mordecai, and Esther, these men and women mourned before the Lord over their own sin, but moreover for the sins of their nations to either avert an impending crisis or procure the favor of God to restore or rebuild the devastation caused by the sins, rebellion, and injustices of the people of God.

Jeremiah is affectionately called "the weeping Prophet" because he wept so much over the sins of the nation and warned its leaders with tears of the impending judgment God was about to bring. In an era when all the other prophets were complicit with the attitude of complacency and debauchery of the people, Jeremiah's voice was not silent and his anguish over the sins and depravity of God's people did not go unnoticed in the corridors of Heaven. Sure enough, judgment came as prophesied:

Lamentations 3:47 – 50: *"Fear and a snare have come upon us, Desolation and destruction. My eyes overflow with rivers of water For the destruction of the daughter of my people. My eyes flow and do not cease, Without* *interruption, Till the LORD from heaven Looks down and sees"*

As we continue to consider this beatitude about mourning or having a godly sorrow over sin, it is helpful to also consider how the people in the Old Testament went about outwardly expressing this attitude. For the most part, it was expressed through fasting, praying, wearing sack cloth and putting ashes over one's head and body. This is where the phrase; "I repent in sack cloth and ashes" comes from. This act of self humiliation and debasement signified one's sincere remorse over sin and desire for repentance and restoration.

When Mordecai, the adopted father of Queen Esther and scribe in the court of King Xerxes, heard about Haman's plot to annihilate the Jewish nation, he did not start a protest march or petition drive to the king who had unconsciously granted Haman's request and signed it into law; not that protests and petition drives don't have their proper place. Mordecai however recognized that this crisis required divine intervention. He therefore positioned himself before God in an attitude of mourning, rending his prestigious attire, as a scribe in the king's court, and putting on sack cloth and ashes before the gate of the palace. Not only did he respond in this manner but the whole Jewish nation also responded in this attitude of mourning when they heard the decree of the king to wipe out their race.

Esther 4:1 – 3: *"When Mordecai learned all that had happened, **he tore his clothes and put on sackcloth and ashes**, and went out into the midst of the city. He* *cried out with a loud and bitter cry. He went as far as the front of the king's gate, for no one might enter the king's gate clothed with sackcloth. And in every province where the king's command and decree arrived, there was* **great mourning among the Jews, with fasting, weeping, and wailing;** *and many lay in sackcloth and ashes"* (Emphasis mine)

Mordecai also encouraged the Queen to use her position with the King for him to overturn his edict. Queen Esther, after her initial reluctance to get involved, called for a period of mourning among the Jews through fasting and prayer. Through these actions the Jewish race was spared of extinction and their enemies eliminated.

When Nehemiah heard about the devastation his people who were left in Jerusalem where facing, and especially that the Temple of the Lord laid in ruins, he immediately went into mourning on the behalf of his nation and people. Even though he himself was in a place of relative comfort and prestige, being the cupbearer of the king, he did not hesitate to identify himself with the sins and needs of his people who were hundreds of miles away. He set himself to fast and pray, and in the process could have jeopardized his own well-being. As the cupbearer of the king, he was not allowed to be forlorn or have a sad countenance in the presence of the king. He was to always maintain a jovial and pleasing expression in the king's presence or risk losing his life.

However, due to his voluntary choice of mourning, he one day came into the presence of the king with a sad and distressful countenance which the king immediately noticed. However, due to the favor of God on Nehemiah's life, instead of punishing him, the king granted him his request to go back home to rebuild the walls of Jerusalem and restore the Temple and the worship of Jehovah.

Nehemiah 1:3 & 4: *"And they said to me, "The survivors who are left from the captivity in the province are there in great distress and reproach. The wall of Jerusalem is also broken down, and its gates are burned with fire." So it was, when I heard these words, that **I sat down and wept, and mourned for many days; I was fasting and praying before the God of heaven"** (Emphasis mine)

As you and I see untold devastation, injustice, immorality, and rebellion in our cities and nation(s) what is our response as children of God? Do we simply bury our heads in the proverbial sand like an ostrich? Do we throw our hands helplessly in the air and do or say nothing? Are we so comfortable in our padded pews within our cozy sanctuaries that we care less about what we see and hear every day around us? Or are we like Jeremiah, Mordecai, Esther, and Nehemiah who refused to be comforted by anything else except God's intervening power, presence, righteousness, mercy, and justice in their lives and that of their communities, cities, and nation. If that is the case, we would have to embrace this beatitude by Jesus to mourn before God over our own sin and that of our cities and nation(s).

In fact, this continues to remain the remedy God has always had for His people in times past and even now. The Book of Joel, in my opinion, is one of the most comprehensive books in the bible that reveals to us about how we ought to respond during national crises; whether they are military, political, economical, or even natural.

In the wake of one of the greatest crises in the history of the nation of Israel where famine, drought, and locusts had obliterated the land of its agricultural sustenance, and just before the impending invasion of the Babylonian Empire under the dictatorship of Nebuchadnezzar; the Prophet Joel spoke forcefully not only about the current and impending crisis, but also about the remedy.

Joel 1:12 – 14: *"The vine has dried up, And the fig tree has withered; The pomegranate tree, The palm tree also, And the apple tree— All the trees of the field are withered; Surely joy has withered away from the sons of men.* **Gird yourselves and lament, you priests; Wail, you who minister before the altar; Come, lie all night in sackcloth,** *You who minister to my God; For the grain offering and the drink offering Are withheld from the house of your God.* **Consecrate a fast, Call a sacred assembly;** *Gather the elders And all the inhabitants of the land Into the house of the LORD your God, And cry out to the LORD"* (Emphasis mine)

Joel 2:11 – 14: *"The LORD gives voice before His army, For His camp is very great; For strong is the One who executes His word. For the day of the LORD is great*

and very terrible; Who can endure it? *"Now,
therefore,"* *says the LORD,* **"Turn to Me with all your
heart, With fasting, with weeping, and with
mourning."** *So rend your heart, and not your garments;
Return to the LORD your God, For He is gracious and
merciful, Slow to anger, and of great kindness; And He
relents from doing harm. Who knows if He will turn
and relent, And leave a blessing behind Him— A grain
offering and a drink offering For the LORD your
God?"* (Emphasis mine)

I am glad that in many nations, especially here in
the United States of America, there is a "National Day of
Prayer". Nevertheless, both you and I know that this day
has now become in many ways, a facade and an exercise in
futility. It has become more of a political event where we
expect the President to attend a function where he makes a
statement he probably did not write himself, while in the
meantime laws are continually being passed that undermine
the very righteousness of the God we claim to be praying
to. I humbly submit that what we don't need is another
religious or political event with the sacred title of "National
Day of Prayer". What we do need is a "National Day of
Mourning"; a solemn day of real repentance and prayer.

This has always been God's way of bringing
genuine revival and restoration to human hearts, cities, and
nations; when we meet in Solemn Assemblies,
acknowledge our sins, repent of them, and ask for God's
intervening mercies upon our lives and our land. That was
His admonishing to His people through the Prophet Joel,

and we will do well in our day to follow that same admonishing.

I was recently delighted when I read how the President of the African nation of Uganda, President Yoweri Museveni, during the celebration of his country's 50th Independence Day Anniversary boldly and publicly repented for the sins of his nation. Below is an excerpt of what he had to say in his prayer, as published in the October 18, 2012 edition of *New Vision*; Uganda's leading daily newspaper:

"...I stand here on my own behalf and on behalf of my predecessors to repent. We ask for your forgiveness. We confess these sins, which have greatly hampered our national cohesion and delayed our political, social and economic transformation. We confess sins of idolatry and witchcraft which are rampant in our land. We confess sins of shedding innocent blood, sins of political hypocrisy, dishonesty, intrigue and betrayal. Forgive us of sins of pride, tribalism and sectarianism; sins of laziness, indifference and irresponsibility; sins of corruption and bribery that have eroded our national resources; sins of sexual immorality, drunkenness and debauchery; sins of un-forgiveness, bitterness, hatred and revenge; sins of injustice, oppression and exploitation; sins of rebellion, insubordination, strife and conflict..."

I believe that this is the kind of bold leadership we need in every nation both spiritually and politically, to acknowledge our waywardness from God's ways and plead for His mercy and blessing over our nations.

Can we truly say that the list of sins the President of Uganda repented of on behalf of his nation are exclusive to that particular nation and not a reflection of our own cultures and societies, especially here in the greatest nation on earth, the United States of America? Don't we also have idols everywhere? We may not be bowing down to physical idols carved out of wood or stone, but we have our own idols we give more allegiance to more than God; namely convenience, entertainment, materialism, and worldly pleasures. We even have the audacity to create a show called *"American Idol"* which millions of viewers, including Christians, can't get enough of. Even in the church we have created idols out of our spiritual leaders and "bow" more to their words than to the infallible Word of God. Some of us wish we had the ability to preach like them or enjoy the fame and fortune they have amassed.

Haven't we also shed innocent blood and thus deserve the wrath of God? You may want to excuse yourself, but when thousands of innocent babies' bloods are shed every day in Abortion Clinics while you and I are silent about it and even support those who pass legislation to legitimize or legalize such abominable practices, are we not also complicit? Shouldn't we also mourn before God for the bloodshed in our streets through murder? How about the sexual immorality, rebellion, oppression, exploitation, and injustice in our bedrooms, classrooms, boardrooms, and courtrooms?

Are we concerned about the racism, sexism, and schisms in our society and even in the Church? When

Sunday, which is the day most people set aside to worship God, is still the most segregated day of the week, isn't it time to acknowledge that something is seriously wrong and apply God's biblical principle to mourn, repent, and ask for His mercy and favor? 2 Chronicles 7:14 is still as relevant today as it was on the day God spoke it to His people through King Solomon during the dedication of the Temple:

2 Chronicles 7:13 – 15: *"When I shut up heaven and there is no rain, or command the locusts to devour the land, or send pestilence among My people, if **My people who are called by My name will humble themselves, and pray and seek My face, and turn from their wicked ways, then I will hear from heaven, and will forgive their sin and heal their land.** Now My eyes will be open and My ears attentive to prayer made in this place"* (Emphasis mine)

God's Comfort:

The blessing or reward for those who mourn, according to the Lord, is that they will be "comforted". The most obvious definition for this is that they will be relieved of their pain and anguish. In other words, when we assume the posture of mourning or godly sorrow over our sins and that of our people and lands, God in turn recompenses us with His goodness and favor. He relents of the judgment due us and refreshes our soul with His presence.

Part of Jesus' mandate as prescribed by Isaiah was that He would recompense those who mourned in Zion with beauty instead of ashes, and the garment of praise instead of a heart of heaviness.

Isaiah 61:2 & 3: *"To proclaim the acceptable year of the LORD, And the day of vengeance of our God;* **To comfort all who mourn, To console those who mourn in Zion,** *To give them beauty for ashes, The oil of joy for mourning, The garment of praise for the spirit of heaviness; That they may be called trees of righteousness, The planting of the LORD, that He may be glorified."'* (Emphasis mine)

Throughout the history of God's people, Israel, when the people mourned over their sins and the sins of their nation and turned back to God, the Lord responded with favor and victory over their enemies, even though they sometimes still had to endure the chastisement of the Lord. As we have discussed already, the mourning attitude of people like Mordecai, Esther, Nehemiah, and Daniel resulted in extreme favor for the people of God and even helped them return from captivity. I also sincerely believe many who escaped the wrath of Nebuchadnezzar, did so because of the mercy of God procured by Jeremiah's mourning.

However, there is another aspect of God's comfort that we need to consider. This may come as a surprise to many when I say that God's comfort is not always comfortable. In fact, He has to often make us uncomfortable in order to give us real comfort. David understood this aspect of God's comfort when he said in Psalms 23:4; one of my favorite Psalms:

Psalms 23:4: *"Yea, though I walk through the valley of the shadow of death, I will fear no evil; For You are with me;* **Your rod and Your staff, they comfort me**" (Emphasis mine)

David gives us two tools God employs to comfort us: His rod, which signifies His correction or discipline; and His staff which signifies His direction and protection. In other words, God uses His rod of correction and staff of direction to provide comfort to His people. Therefore, these two things serve as the boundaries God uses to allow His River of grace and comfort to flow.

In an era where convenience and ease is the goal of many, even in the church, we need to be aware that God will often put us in uncomfortable situations in order to bring us to His desired destiny for us. Most of the calamities the people of Israel faced as a result of their rebellion against God in pursuing after other gods (conveniences) were God employing His "rod" to eventually cause His people

GOD'S COMFORT IS NOT ALWAYS COMFORTABLE

to mourn so He could give them true comfort. In order to avoid the rod of God, we need to refuse any comforts that make us comfortable in our sinful condition and apathetic attitude and response to God's presence and commands. His comfort is a thousand times better than any false comfort this world has to offer because His lasts for eternity, while worldly comforts are fleeting and devastating.

The Blessed Life

Chapter 3

MEEKNESS: *Strength under Control*

Blessed are the meek: for they shall inherit the earth
(Matthew 5:5)

JESUS in His sermon proceeds to discuss the beatitude, 'meekness' which I believe is one of the most difficult and yet rewarding attributes God expects us to have. However, it is the one attitude least exhibited among Christians in my opinion, let alone unbelievers. It does not mean it is impossible to attain, but it does mean it demands our particular attention.

Walking in meekness is somewhat similar to being poor in spirit. They are different however in the sense that being poor in spirit means you acknowledge your spiritual lack before God and the great need for His grace and mercy. Meekness, on the other hand, involves the acknowledgment of our lack before people; our indebtedness to God for the resources that He gives us; and our acknowledgement of His ownership of those resources.

> **MEEKNESS DEMANDS THAT WE USE OUR RESOURCES TO SERVE OTHERS**

Meekness therefore demands that we use these resources, including our authority, to serve others with a Servant's heart.

It is almost unheard of for anyone to claim of themselves that they are meek or humble without sounding and projecting the opposite. However, with clarity and boldness Moses inserted in his writing of the Pentateuch that he was the meekest man on earth.

Numbers 12:3: *"(Now **the man Moses** was **very humble [meek]**, more than all men who were on the face of the earth)"* (Emphasis mine)

Some have suggested that Joshua, Moses' assistant, was the one who inserted this parenthesis describing the character of Moses. Nevertheless, it is one of the greatest statements of character traits that anyone could receive. Why is it that Moses was considered the meekest man on earth?

If we take a cursory look at the life of Moses, we immediately attest that he did not begin as a meek man. He was rather proud. Who could blame him? Born as a Jew, but raised as a Prince in the Palace of Pharaoh, the King of the greatest kingdom on earth, Egypt. Moses had everything he could possibly desire. The Bible says that Moses was *"learned in all the wisdom of the Egyptians and was mighty in words and in deeds"* (**Acts 7:22**). Wealth, power, fame, and security were at his disposal; while his kindred people, the Israelites were in bondage, poverty, and without any security while they were praying and waiting for God to send their deliverer.

After Moses eventually discovered who he really was while he was still in the palace, he expected the children of Israel to acknowledge him as their deliverer. He took matters into his own hands which led him to become a fugitive after he fled the land for killing an Egyptian who he found abusing an Israelite slave.

His forty years wilderness experience in the household of Jethro was the school God took him to humble him and remove all the boastfulness, pride, and anger of Egypt from him. When he left Egypt, he was a mighty man of words and deeds; but after his sojourn in the wilderness, he had become a man of stammering lips and no power (of himself). He had also become a man who was aware of his utter dependence on Jehovah, even though he did not know Him until his burning bush encounter.

When Moses returned to Egypt to face his nemesis Pharaoh and deliver God's people, he was a man who was "poor in spirit" and meek. He acknowledged before

Pharaoh and the Israelites that he was nothing, and could do nothing except by the unction and direction of God. He was the total opposite of Pharaoh, who being a mere mortal, considered himself to be a god. In spite of all the authority and miraculous power God granted to him; and above all, the face-to-face encounters he had with God, Moses remained as humble and meek as anyone could possibly be.

His meekness was really highlighted when he had every right and opportunity to allow God to destroy His people in the wilderness for murmuring against Him and the leader He had provided for them. During every incidence in which God was prepared to annihilate His people, Moses stood before God on behalf of the people to intercede. He used his position and authority not to enforce God's judgment against the people but rather to defend and avert the utmost punishment God had planned for 'the Children of Israel'.

On one particular occasion when the people of Israel had rebelled against God by worshipping the molten calf Aaron had fashioned while Moses was on Mount Sinai for 40 days receiving the Ten Commandments, God intended to totally wipe out the entire nation and begin afresh with Moses.

Exodus 32:9-10: *"And the LORD said to Moses, "I have seen this people, and indeed it is a stiff-necked people! Now therefore, let Me alone, that My wrath may burn hot against them and I may consume them. And I will make of you a great nation.""*

Many of us today would have jumped at this offer from God. Imagine having the power to endorse God's judgment and in so doing you would become the father of 'a people or ethnic group'. The opportunity to become the father of God's people would be too enticing to refuse. After all, those stiff-necked people did not appreciate anything Moses had done for them nor did they appreciate all that he had endured because of them. They were in it for themselves and had caused him much disappointment so why not allow God to go ahead and wipe them out and begin a new blood line. This was a big deal!

If Moses accepted God's proposal, there would no longer be the "Children of Israel", but instead the "Children of Moses". Additionally, we would no longer refer to God as the "God of Abraham, Isaac, and Jacob" but rather the "God of Moses".

However, without hesitation Moses stood between God and the people and pleaded on their behalf. He rejected God's offer outright, but instead appealed to God's faithfulness in upholding His covenant with His people. And God acquiesced.

Exodus 32:11-14: *"Then Moses pleaded with the LORD his God, and said: "LORD, why does Your wrath burn hot against Your people whom You have brought out of the land of Egypt with great power and with a mighty hand? ... Turn from Your fierce wrath, and relent from this harm to Your people. Remember Abraham, Isaac, and Israel, Your servants, to whom You swore by Your* *own self, and said to them, 'I will multiply your descendants as the stars of heaven; and all this land that I have spoken of I give to your descendants, and they shall inherit it forever.' "So the LORD relented from the harm which He said He would do to His people"*

Rather than using his position of power and authority for his own self preservation and advancement, he used it to save the people and more importantly to preserve God's integrity and overall purpose. Moses was meek indeed!

The Meekness of David:

We see this attitude or attribute of meekness also in the life of King David. David did not only acknowledge openly his poverty of spirit towards God; he also acknowledged his lack before the people he served. With the exception of his episode with Bathsheba and all the things he did to try to cover his sin, He used his power, authority, and resources to serve God's purposes and people in his generation. This was his desire and focus, to be meek and humble before God and His people. This attitude is what made him even more contrite in repentance when the Prophet Nathan confronted him with his sin of adultery and murder.

Throughout the story of David's life, we see a man who did not take undue advantage of his position, privilege and prestige to promote himself at the expense of others. To the contrary, we encounter a man who fully understood that he was nothing and had nothing except by the hand of God and hence, committed himself to serve his people and generation according to the will of God in meekness and humility.

Act 13:36: *"For David, **after he had served his own generation by the will of God**, fell asleep, was buried with his fathers, and saw corruption "* (Emphasis mine)

The Lord Has Need of This Donkey:

It was a day in 1995 in Accra, Ghana that I heard the voice of God say to me, "The Lord has need of this donkey." I did not understand what this meant, but knew that I had heard from God. During this period of my life, I was just getting to know the Lord in a real way. I hardly knew much about the Holy Spirit, let alone the voice of God even though I had been raised up in religion. I hardly read the Bible, partly because the church denomination I grew up in never really encouraged the congregation to study the Word for themselves. We carried and knew more about what was in the hymn book than the Bible. The studying and preaching of the Word was the responsibility of the Priest and maybe a few others. And so, when I heard this statement from the Lord, I had no biblical reference to judge the veracity of God's voice.

> GOD IS CALLING HIS PEOPLE TO A LIFESTYLE OF MEEKNESS

Since it was close to Easter, I was reading the Gospels concerning the "Passion of Christ" and came across this passage in Matthew:

45

Matthew 21:1-3: *"Now when they drew near Jerusalem, and came to Bethphage, at the Mount of Olives, then Jesus sent two disciples, saying to them, "Go into the village opposite you, and immediately you will find a donkey tied, and a colt with her. Loose them and bring them to Me. And if anyone says anything to you, you shall say, 'The Lord has need of them,' and immediately he will send them.""* (Emphasis mine)

I was excited because I knew instantly this was what the Lord had spoken to me earlier. I still did not have a clue immediately of what it meant or what the Lord expected me to do with the small phrase I heard but at least I knew I was not crazy and just hearing things. This gave me more confidence in my relationship with the Holy Spirit in seeking Him for wisdom and revelation in His Word, and He always comes through. He prompted me to continue to read and meditate on that chapter and with the combination of other scriptures the message became and still is becoming clearer. In essence, God was calling me and His people to a lifestyle of meekness and humility.

The question we need to ask as we read Matthew 21 is, "why didn't Jesus request for a horse but rather sought for a donkey?" After all, He was coming into town as the King of the Jews. In those days, Kings didn't ride on donkeys, they rode on horses. In fact, verses 4 and 5 suggest that it surprised the people to see Him riding on a donkey instead of a horse, but realized He was fulfilling a prophecy by Zechariah:

Zechariah 9:9: *""Rejoice greatly, O daughter of Zion! Shout, O daughter of Jerusalem! Behold, your King is coming to you; He is just and having salvation, **Lowly and riding on a donkey,** A colt, the foal of a donkey"* (Emphasis mine)

Matthew 21:4 & 5: *"All this was done that it might be fulfilled which was spoken by the prophet, saying: "tell the daughter of Zion, 'behold, your king is coming to you, **lowly, and sitting on a donkey,** a colt, the foal of a donkey.' ""* (Emphasis mine)

The reason Jesus rode on a donkey rather than on a horse is because He wanted to display one of His most important character traits: meekness. Jesus exhibited meekness in His life and ministry on earth more than any other person. Among the many attributes and characteristics we can project onto Jesus, the one character trait He boldly claimed about Himself above all was His meekness, lowliness, or humility. Nowhere do we really hear Jesus say about Himself that "I am loving", though we know He absolutely is; or that "I am faithful" even though He definitely is. However, when it came time for Jesus to describe Him-self he proclaimed and explained in Matthew 11:28-30 the essence of who He truly was.

Matthew 11:28-30: *"Come to Me, all you who labor and are heavy laden, and I will give you rest. Take My yoke upon you and **learn from Me, for I am gentle and lowly in heart,** and you will find rest for your souls. For*

47

My yoke is easy and My burden is light" (Emphasis mine)

The greatest attribute Jesus wants us to learn from Him above everything else is meekness. Paul tells us in his Epistle to the Philippians that we should have the same mindset that Jesus had when He voluntarily set aside His divinity to come and redeem fallen man:

Philippians 2:5-9: *"**Let this mind be in you which was also in Christ Jesus**, who, being in the form of God, did not consider it robbery to be equal with God, **but made Himself of no reputation, taking the form of a bond-servant**, and coming in the likeness of men. And being found in appearance as a man, **He humbled Himself** and became obedient to the point of death, even the death of the cross. Therefore God also has highly exalted Him and given Him the name which is above every name"* (Emphasis mine)

In order to prove that this attitude of meekness was not only in display on earth at His first Advent, but rather is a vital part of the character of the God-head eternally, Jesus will rule the Nations at His glorious Second Advent in righteousness, justice, and meekness.

Psalms 45:3-4: *"Girt Your sword upon Your thigh, O Mighty One, With Your glory and Your majesty. And in Your majesty ride prosperously because of **truth, humility, and righteousness**; And Your right hand shall teach You awesome things"* (Emphasis mine)

We know that God the Father is meek because Jesus is the expressed *"image of the invisible God"* (**Colossians 1:15**). He came to express the character of the Father and therefore, if Jesus exhibited meekness, that must be the Father's character also. Secondly, it is impossible for God to make a demand of you and me that He Himself is not already abiding by. He leads us by example.

Jesus rode triumphantly into Jerusalem on what has become to be known as "Palm Sunday" on a donkey to portray to everyone not only who He was, but also the kind of people He seeks to use to transform cities and nations. He projected His character of meekness through the donkey. In other words He is saying to His people that if they want Him to "ride" on them triumphantly to reform their generation and transform their regions, then they will have to become like donkeys and not horses. It is my humble observation and opinion that many in the Kingdom of God today, and especially in the Ministry, would rather be horses than donkeys.

Donkey or Horse: Which Way?

These two animals are from the same animal family and have many similarities especially in their external features. However, there is a great deal of differences between them in terms of their character and how they respond to human authority. Let's just take a brief look at some of the differences; and then hopefully make the necessary adjustments in our attitudes through prayer to become like donkeys and not horses.

First, let's take a look at the horse. These creatures are big, fast, intelligent, and beautiful. As a result of these qualities, they are also proud, stubborn, and can be deadly if agitated. I used to be quite a big fan of horseracing. What really fascinates me about the sport is the creative names the horses are known by. It is however strange that hardly anyone knows the names of the Jockeys that ride these popular horses. No one really goes to the "Kentucky Derby" to watch the jockeys? The real attention is on the horses! It seems as if the horses also know it and love it; basking in all the attention and affection thrown their way. The jockeys are almost insignificant and invisible to the viewer, except perhaps when their horse wins the race.

This analogy is similar to what goes on in the Kingdom of God. There are many 'horses' in the Kingdom who are doing great things for the Lord either in ministry or in the market place, but no one really knows or recognizes the Person who has trained them, blessed them, and is directing them. They gladly receive and bask in the accolades and the praises of men without sincerely and forcefully deflecting the praise and the glory to the One who is really due such honor. Their 'performance' and 'accomplishments' become the yardstick by which they judge themselves and others judge them, whether they are successful or not. This attitude is prideful, when we refuse to truly deflect the praise of men onto Jesus. We need to know and let others know that we are nothing and can do nothing without the Divine influence and empowerment from the Lord (**John 15:6**). We need to stop acting as if we could accomplish anything by our own power and ingenuity.

This is the exact attitude Paul admonishes us to take when he wrote to the Church at Corinth. There was so much division in the church due to the rise of different factions who held special allegiances to the various spiritual leaders who had impacted their lives; instead of focusing more on the Lordship of Jesus. Some claimed they were for Paul, while others were for Peter and others for Apollos (1 Cor. 1:11 – 13). This sounds exactly like what is going on in the 21st Century Church, except on a larger and global scale. The divisions in the Body of Christ today is exacerbated as many "Christians" put more emphasis on their denominational affiliation than on their affiliation to the Body of Christ as a whole; while many more speak more about their bishops, pastors, spiritual leaders or "fathers" and hold them in higher regard than the Lord Jesus Himself.

Paul's response to this travesty was to appeal to the Corinthians (and to us) to first of all stop placing undue praise and recognition, reserved only for the Lord, to those He has anointed and sent to minister the gospel. Secondly to all of us who operate in the ministry, he admonishes us to walk in meekness, readily acknowledging the One who anointed us and graced us with our gifts and talents.

1 Corinthians 3:5: *"Who then is Paul, and who is Apollos, but ministers through whom you believed, as the Lord gave to each one?"*

51

1 Corinthians 4:6 & 7: *"Now these things, brethren, I have figuratively transferred to myself and Apollos for your sakes, that you may learn in us not to think beyond what is written, **that none of you may be puffed up on behalf of one against the other**. For who makes you differ from another? **And what do you have that you did not receive? Now if you did indeed receive it, why do you boast as if you had not received it?**"* (Emphasis mine)

Even the Lord Jesus recognized this concept during His earthly ministry, and made sure He deflected any praise that came His way to His Father when He healed the sick. Many times after He healed or delivered someone from demonic oppression or possession, He told them to either not mention it to anyone except the priests who would confirm the healing or go and tell of what God the Father (not Jesus) had done for them. For example, after He delivered the Legion possessed man, His directive to Him was profound, since the people in the town did not want anything to do with Him:

Mark 5:19-20: *"However, Jesus did not permit him, but said to him, "Go home to your friends, and **tell them what great things the Lord has done for you**, and how He has had compassion on you." And he departed and **began to proclaim in Decapolis all that Jesus had done for him**; and all marveled"* (Emphasis mine)

Jesus clearly deflected the praise to His Father who had sent and anointed Him. However, the man who was delivered clearly recognized the role Jesus played in his deliverance and couldn't help but give Him the credit and praise also. Today many preachers have the pride and audacity to ask and expect people God has used them to help to go tell others what they (the preacher) has done for them. Some even go so far as to claim ownership of other people's 'success' because they might have trained or helped them in some fashion at some stage of their lives. If we would be humble and meek like Jesus, we would have to cease expecting and claiming the accolades that will surely come to us as a result of the grace God poured out of our lives to bless His people. When they do come, we need to sincerely, humbly, and forcefully return it to the 'Jockey' who is riding on us. His Name is Jesus!

There is a popular saying that "you can make the horse go to the river, but you can't make it drink the water". The stubbornness of the horse is the main reason they require a bit and bridle. Without it, they cannot be controlled or directed appropriately; going in the direction they choose.

Psalm 32:8-9: *"I will instruct you and teach you in the way you should go; I will guide you with My eye.* ***Do not be like the horse*** *or like the mule, Which have no understanding,* ***Which must be harnessed with bit and bridle****, Else they will not come near you"* (Emphasis mine)

The reason the bit and bridle is so effective in leading and redirecting the horse is because it causes pain in the mouth of the horse which then causes it to turn in that direction to relieve the pain. The Bible clearly admonishes us in the scripture just referenced to let go of any horse-like tendencies and attitudes if we want to be led and directed by God. You don't need God's bit and bridle to guide you, because it causes unnecessary pain. Don't allow your intelligence, beauty, strength, position, quickness, charisma, etc., to cause you to become proud like a horse. God is not looking for horses; He is after donkeys!

Ecclesiastics 9:11: *"I returned and saw under the sun that— The race is not to the swift, Nor the battle to the strong, Nor bread to the wise, Nor riches to men of understanding, Nor favor to men of skill; But time and chance happen to them all"*

Jeremiah 9:23 & 24: *"Thus says the LORD: "Let not the wise man glory in his wisdom, Let not the mighty man glory in his might, Nor let the rich man glory in his riches; But let him who glories glory in this, That he understands and knows Me, That I am the LORD, exercising lovingkindness, judgment, and righteousness in the earth. For in these I delight," says the LORD"*

Unlike the horse, there is not much externally to be desired in a donkey. They are not very big; not fast or agile; don't look smart; and definitely not beautiful. However, what they lack in external qualities they more than compensate with internal desirable qualities. Donkeys, unlike horses, don't need a bit and bridle to make them go in the direction they are required. They may not be fast and agile like the horse, but they will go the distance you want them to go without complaint or resistance. Though they may not look smart, they are very sensitive and intelligent, like Balaam's donkey in **Numbers 22**. Above all, they will not 'steal' the glory that should go to the One that is riding on them. The donkey is content to give attention and prominence to its rider. They

> THE DONKEY IS CONTENT TO GIVE ATTENTION AND PROMINENCE TO ITS RIDER

take the attitude of John the Baptist, who famously replied to those who expected him to be upset when they told him that Jesus was drawing more followers than him:

John 3:29-30: *"He who has the bride is the bridegroom; but the friend of the bridegroom, who stands and hears him, rejoices greatly because of the bridegroom's voice. Therefore this joy of mine is fulfilled. **He must increase, but I must decrease"*** (Emphasis mine)

As the Lord has continued to impress my heart with this revelation, I realize that meekness or humility is the greatest attribute anyone can possibly attain. Jesus is beginning to find true 'donkeys' in these last days, who He will ride into neighborhoods, cities, and nations to "move" them just as the city of Jerusalem was "moved" at the site of the King of Kings riding on a donkey.

Matthew 21:10: *"And when He had come into Jerusalem, **all the city was moved**, saying, "Who is this?""* (Emphasis mine)

For all who think that there are no rewards for being a donkey, you should read Matthew 21:10 again. The greatest reward and honor for me is having the Lord of Glory choosing to ride on me triumphantly, to accomplish His purposes. However, there are other rewards. Even though the people laid their clothes and branches out for Jesus, it was the donkey which

> GOD IS NOT LOOKING FOR HORSES, BUT DONKEYS

actually walked on them. People will seek to bless Jesus by blessing you as they see Jesus fully exalted and expressed in your life. You wouldn't have to ask or demand it, only stay meek and let the glory of the risen Lord shine unhindered through you.

Meekness: Strength under Control

One of the ways we exhibit meekness is when we show restraint in the face of opposition, resistance, or false accusation. Even though we might have the power and the "right" to respond and react with anger and retaliation, we should employ self-control in order to hold our peace and instead respond in love and grace. When people operate in a spirit of self-control; many people mistake their "meekness" as "weakness". On the contrary, it is the greatest strength one possesses, because instead of taking matters into your own hand, you relinquish judgment into the capable Hands of God. In fact, though it looks like weakness, it releases the strength of God; and also accomplishes His righteousness.

Throughout His Sermon on the Mount, Jesus stressed this attitude of restraint on the part of His disciples who He knew would face persecution and opposition. He discussed how important it was to pray for those who may despitefully use you; not repaying evil for evil, but instead, doing good to those who would do otherwise to you.

The person, who takes matters into his or her own hands to retaliate for offenses committed against them, is one who does not trust in God's judicial system. I refer to such a person as a "spiritual vigilante". We need to therefore trust in the Lord when we encounter resistance, opposition, and false accusations; and respond in meekness.

Romans 12:19-21: *"Beloved, do not avenge yourselves, but rather give place to wrath; for it is written, "vengeance is mine, i will repay," says the Lord. Therefore "if your enemy is hungry, feed him; if he is thirsty, give him a drink; for in so doing you will heap coals of fire on his head." Do not be overcome by evil, but overcome evil with good"*

James 1:19-21: *"So then, my beloved brethren, let every man be swift to hear, slow to speak, slow to wrath; for the wrath of man does not produce the righteousness of God. Therefore lay aside all filthiness and overflow of wickedness, and **receive with meekness** the implanted word, which is able to save your souls"* (Emphasis mine)

The greatest place we see the Son of God exhibit His meekness is on the cross of Calvary. Jesus had all the power to summon legions of Angels to come assist and deliver Him from the cruel hands of the Roman soldiers who were encouraged and incited by the Jewish leaders. Instead He held His peace and submitted Himself to their acts of unmitigated violence and verbal abuse. In His dialogue with Pilate, the Governor of Judah who thought he had ultimate authority over Jesus, Jesus made him to understand that his power was limited to God's and he was not doing Jesus a favor by withholding his sentence.

John 19:10-11: *"Then Pilate said to Him, "Are You not speaking to me? Do You not know that I have power to crucify You, and power to release You?" Jesus answered, "You could have no power at all against Me unless it had been given you from above"*

Also in the Garden of Gethsemane when Judas Iscariot led the mob to arrest Jesus, one of His disciples stepped up to defend him and in so doing slashed off the ear of one of the High Priest's servants. Instead of applauding the disciple, as some would, Jesus instead rebuked him, laid His hand on the servant's ear and healed him. That is meekness at its highest expression because Jesus had been wronged and thus, had a 'right' to retaliate. However, Jesus restrained Himself from doing harm and even helped to restore the person perpetrating the wrong actions against Him. If we were placed in that same scenario; could we portray the meekness coupled with mercy that Jesus so wonderfully showcased?

Luke 22:50-51: *"And one of them struck the servant of the high priest and cut off his right ear. But Jesus answered and said, "Permit even this."* And He touched his ear and healed him"*

We need to walk in meekness towards one another in all our relationships. I believe one reason for so much heartache in marriages that ultimately have led to many divorces is because of the spouses' refusal to walk in meekness towards each other. When husbands use their authority to mistreat their wives, they expose their weakness and insecurity.

The husband is supposed to be the strong man, the defender, and the one who offers a covering for his household. He should not therefore be the one who "enforces" his authority by disrespecting, mistreating, or abusing his wife and/or children. I can't stress this point enough: the strong husband and father is the one who through meekness serves his family because he is very much secure in who he is. He is the one who treats his bride like Jesus does His: cherishing, nourishing,

> MEEKNESS IS NOT WEAKNESS; BUT STRENGTH UNDER CONTROL

protecting, providing, and above all serving her. He does not mind picking up a "towel" so that he can wash the feet of those he has authority over, like Jesus did for His disciples. He understands and knows that meekness is not weakness, but rather meekness is strength under control.

This ultimately goes for all leaders whether in the ministry or in the market place. The strength of your leadership is your willingness to serve, with meekness, those you have oversight.

Inheriting the Earth:

The reward associated with walking in meekness, according to Jesus, is "inheriting the earth". This is a profound promise! What does it mean to inherit the earth?

It is important to remember that the purpose for us to become meek like the donkey is so that the Master may 'ride' on us to bring regional transformation to our neighborhoods, cities, and nation(s). Being meek therefore attracts the grace and power of God to cause us to have influence and impact on the earth right now.

1 Peter 5:5 & 6: *"Likewise you younger people, submit yourselves to your elders. Yes, all of you be submissive to one another, and **be clothed with humility**, for "God resists the proud, but gives grace to the humble." Therefore humble yourselves under the mighty hand of God, that He may exalt you in due time"* (Emphasis mine)

However, the fullness of this promise and reward will be fulfilled when Jesus comes back to set up His eternal Kingdom on earth. This means that having an eternal perspective is the greatest motivation to living a life of meekness now.

It is also important to understand that God's original plan and intentions concerning earth has not changed. In the beginning, God created earth for man; and even though Satan's deception temporarily caused man to lose his inheritance, God through the "Last Adam" has every intention to restore earth to its original owners: you and I.

The extent to which each of us will have authority and dominion on the restored earth under the direct leadership of Jesus in eternity will vary based on our lifestyle now. Those who have used the position, authority, and influence God has graciously bestowed on them now to 'lord' it over others for their own personal gain; and to enhance their own egos and selfish-ambitions will be surprised to find they have less influence in the Kingdom of God, especially in the age to come. However, those who have pursued God with a spirit of meekness, using their resources to serve others sincerely will have a prominent role in Christ's Kingdom on earth in His triumphant return.

Interestingly this goes for all the Beatitudes seeing that the rewards are magnified and completely fulfilled in the eternal Kingdom of God, even though we experience so much in the here and now. In other words, striving by God's grace to live the 'Sermon on the Mount' lifestyle is like an internship on earth now for what our life is

> WE ARE IN TRAINING FOR REIGNING

going to be like for eternity. We are basically in training for reigning. Fifty to seventy years of earthly internship for an eternity full of the pleasures of God. Jesus said to the disciples in His discourse that fulfilling the requirements of His sermon meant greatness in His Kingdom; both now and in eternity.

Matthew 5:19: *"Whoever therefore breaks one of the least of these commandments, and teaches men so, shall be called least in the kingdom of heaven; but whoever does and teaches them,* **he shall be called great in the kingdom of heaven***"* (Emphasis mine)

Chapter 4

HUNGER AND THIRST: *Your Divine Escorts*

*Blessed are they which do hunger and thirst after
righteousness: for they shall be filled   (Matthew 5:6)*

WHEN you are hungry you seek for food. When you
are thirsty you seek for water. Seeking or pursuit is therefore the ultimate sign or proof of desire. When you therefore are hungry and thirsty for God you will seek or pursue
Him, His Kingdom, and His righteousness, (His way of
doing things).

Spiritual hunger drives you to the place of prayer,
fasting, and the Word of God to receive the deep things of
God that will only satisfy the human soul. *"Deep calls onto*

deep", the Bible says in Ps. 42:7. Your deep desire for spiritual fulfillment will cry out to God's deep reservoir of spiritual fulfillment. Hunger and thirst are therefore the divine escorts into the deep things of God.

Righteousness: God's Way of Doing Things

There are two intertwining truths about the righteousness of God. They are His imputed righteousness which is our legal position in Christ; and His imparted righteousness which is our living condition in Christ. The former speaks of our right-standing in God while the latter speaks of our right-living before God.

We are not and cannot hunger and thirst for more of God's imputed righteousness, since that was already settled in full when we received Jesus as Lord and Savior. This righteousness is perfect. It cannot be improved upon. There is nothing you and I can do to increase it or decrease it. However we are to hunger and thirst for more of God's imparted righteousness which affects our

> THE PROOF OF DESIRE IS IN SEEKING OR PURSUIT

living condition before our righteous God. Our sincere desire to be more like Him in prayer, fasting, and study of His word releases grace in our hearts to think like Him and live like Him; doing things His way.

One of the greatest commandments Jesus gave during His Sermon on the Mount can be found in Matthew 6:33.

Matthew 6:33: *"But seek first the kingdom of God and His righteousness, and all these things shall be added to you"*

This scripture can easily be rendered, *"But seek first the domain of God, and His way of doing things..."* (Paraphrase).

Remember that Jesus was addressing the attitude of His disciples who lived in a Roman controlled culture, influenced by a hedonistic mindset. He was confronting their sense of insecurity in terms of how they would be sustained; thus, putting all their pursuits and efforts into fulfilling legitimate desires, but in a selfish and ungodly way.

Matthew 6:24 – 32: *"No one can serve two masters; for either he will hate the one and love the other, or else he will be loyal to the one and despise the other. **You cannot serve God and mammon.** "Therefore I say to you, do not worry about your life, what you will eat or what you will drink; nor about your body, what you will put on. Is not life more than food and the body more than clothing... "Therefore do not worry, saying, 'What shall we eat?' or 'What shall we drink?' or 'What shall we wear?' **For after all these things the Gentiles seek.** For your heavenly Father knows that you need all these things"* (Emphasis mine)

He made it clear that this attitude of putting a lot of energy and effort into amassing material possessions was

65

something the Gentiles or Heathen (those outside the covenant of God) do; because they operate under a worldly sys-tem or kingdom which is foreign to the way God operates in His Kingdom. Jesus was thus challenging His disciples to have a new mindset; a mindset that was congruent to the principles of God's Kingdom which if they followed would release all of the resources in His Kingdom for their benefit. To seek His Kingdom and His righteousness therefore meant that they were to pursue the ruler-ship of God in their lives and to hunger and thirst after God's way of doing things in His Kingdom.

This is similar to what God spoke to His people Israel thousands of years earlier through the Prophet Isaiah. In Isaiah 55, there is an interesting message God gave to the Prophet concerning the kind of relationship His people had with Him; and the kind of relationship He wanted to have with them.

Isaiah 55:8 & 9: *""For My thoughts are not your thoughts, Nor are your ways My ways," says the LORD."For as the heavens are higher than the earth, So are My ways higher than your ways, And My thoughts than your thoughts"*

I believe this is one of the most misunderstood and misinterpreted passages in the bible. Many in the pulpit and pew alike have suggested based on this scripture that we cannot know or understand the ways of God. You hear this fallacy often quoted especially during times of tragedy. We use it to comfort a family who has unexpectedly lost a loved one, trying to console them with something along this line: "You know God's ways are not our ways, so we can't understand why this happened; so we shouldn't question God. After all, God knows best". During devastations, such as natural disasters like Hurricane Katrina in the Gulf Coast; and school massacres like those in Columbine, Colorado, or in New Port, Connecticut when people don't understand the reason for such tragedies, they ask why God would allow such a thing. I have sometimes heard uninformed spiritual leaders use this scripture as a 'cop-out' that since "God's ways are higher than ours," we cannot understand why such evil continues to rampage our society.

This unfortunate explanation has been perpetrated by well meaning Christians for so long and has inadvertently caused many to resign themselves to the notion that we are incapable of knowing or understanding God's way of thinking or doing things; which actually represents His righteousness. I am not in any way suggesting that we become "equal" to God in His knowledge and understanding. He is Omniscient (ALL knowing), we are not; He is Omnipresent (ALL present), we are not; and He is Omnipotent (ALL powerful), and we are definitely not.

Perhaps the scripture more appropriate for us to use to excuse ourselves from knowing God's ways is the one Paul used to explain the depth of the understanding and know-ledge of God; which we mortals have no capacity to comprehend:

Romans 11:33 & 34: *"Oh, the depth of the riches both of the wisdom and knowledge of God! How unsearchable are His judgments and His ways past finding out! "For who has known the mind of the Lord? Or who has become his counselor?"*

Let me assure you that God intends for you and I to know His ways and thoughts. His message through His Prophet Isaiah should be understood more as an indictment on the people of God, rather than as a statement of fact and intention.

According to Isaiah, the reason God's ways and thoughts are higher than ours is because of our wickedness and unrighteousness respectively. His admonishing therefore to His people is for us to forsake our own ways of wickedness and our own thoughts of unrighteousness in order to have or receive the ways (righteousness) and thoughts of God.

Is. 55:6 -8: *"Seek the LORD while He may be found, Call upon Him while He is near.* **Let the wicked forsake his way, And the unrighteous man his thoughts;** *Let him return to the LORD, And He will have mercy on him; And to our God, For He will abundantly pardon.* **"For My thoughts are not your thoughts, Nor are your ways My ways,"** *says the LORD"* (Emphasis mine)

It is worth repeating that the reason why God says the thoughts and ways of His people were contrary to His was because they were not actively seeking Him; (hungering

68

and thirsting) to know His thoughts and His ways. Therefore, they had become so disconnected from Him that they were not recognizable as the triumphant people of God. Does that sound familiar?

The Apostle Paul also confirms this truth about how we are supposed to know and are entitled to know God's thoughts and ways in his letter to the Corinthians. He boldly declares that we who are redeemed by the blood of the Lamb have the mind of Christ which means we also have the mind of God.

> LET HIS WAYS BECOME YOUR WAYS; AND HIS THOUGHTS YOUR THOUGHTS

1 Cor. 2:16: *"For "who has known the mind of the lord that he may instruct him?" **But we have the mind of Christ"*** (Emphasis mine)

David's Hunger and Thirst:

David gives us insight into his primary focus and mission in life when he declares in Psalms 27:4:

Psalms 27:4: *"One thing have I desired of the LORD, that will I seek after; that I may dwell in the house of the LORD all the days of my life, to behold the beauty of the LORD, and to enquire in his temple"*

David's one singular desire or thirst in life was to be in the presence of God, and also to become like God by beholding Him constantly.

Psalms 16:8: *"I have set the LORD always before me: because he is at my right hand, I shall not be moved"* (Emphasis mine)

Without going into all that depth about what it means to "behold the beauty of the LORD," it is clear David understood this simple, but profound principle: what you constantly behold, you will also become. His ultimate hunger and thirst was to become like God; to know His ways and thus to be righteous. As you can also notice, it was not enough for him to only desire, but the proof of that desire was his decision to also passionately seek after His ways.

Psalms 63:1-8: *"O God, You are my God; Early will I seek You; My soul thirsts for You; My flesh longs for You In a dry and thirsty land Where there is no water. So I have looked for You in the sanctuary, To see Your power and Your glory...My soul follows close behind You; Your right hand upholds me"*

David's desire to know God's ways is a primary theme in most of his prayer dialogue with God, found throughout the Psalms.

Psalm 25:4 & 5: *"Show me Your ways, O LORD; Teach me Your paths. Lead me in Your truth and teach me, For You are the God of my salvation; On You I wait all the day"*

Psalm 119:1 – 8: *"Blessed are the undefiled in the way, Who walk in the law of the LORD! Blessed are those* *who keep His testimonies, **Who seek Him with the whole heart!** They also do no iniquity; **They walk in His ways.** You have commanded us To keep Your precepts diligently. **Oh, that my ways were directed To keep Your statutes!** Then I would not be ashamed, When I look into all Your commandments. I will praise You with uprightness of heart, **When I learn Your righteous judgments.** I will keep Your statutes; Oh, do not forsake me utterly!"* (Emphasis mine)

Show me Your Glory:

This attitude of David brings to mind another patriarch, who also made it his singular quest to know God's ways. Almost everyone can recount one of the greatest requests made by a man to God; when Moses stood before the Lord and asked Him: *"show me Your glory"* (**Exodus 33:18**). What many fail to see or appreciate is what Moses asked the Lord just before his now famous request. Before he asked the Lord to show him His glory, he first asked Him to show him His ways:

Exodus 33:13: *"Now therefore, I pray, if I have found grace in Your sight, **show me now Your way, that I may know You** and that I may find grace in Your sight. And consider that this nation is Your people"* (Emphasis mine)

What we need to realize is that prior to this request, Moses had already experienced the power and glory of God like no other human had and probably will. He had seen

God rain down ten plagues to destroy Egypt; he had seen the Red Sea part so that Israel could pass through on dry ground, while swallowing up the pursuing Egyptian army; and he had spent forty days and nights in the very glorious presence of God receiving the ten commandments written on tables of stone with the fiery finger of God.

Hence when Moses had the opportunity to ask God to show him His glory, he was not requesting another show of demonstrative power from God. That is why his prior request in verse 13 is the key to unlocking what Moses was really seeking from the Lord. God also knew exactly what His servant was after

> **WHAT YOU CONSTANTLY BEHOLD, YOU WILL ALSO BECOME**

more than anything: He was after God's ways. He was after His righteousness. In essence, he wanted to know God; and in knowing Him he would then become like him in thought and in deeds.

When his request was granted and He was summoned by God to spend another forty days and nights in His presence, God passed before Him and he saw His back side. When he returned to the camp the children of Israel could not steadfastly behold his countenance because it shined like the glory of God they had also seen and been afraid of. Moses had become like the One He beheld!

Become Like Him:

Jesus lets us know that the reward or blessing for hungering and thirsting after righteousness is that we will

72

be filled. When we sincerely seek after God to know His ways, we are drawn automatically into His magnificent presence where He fills us with His thoughts and His ways, thus enabling us to walk in His righteousness and also do His works.

King David summarizes the difference between Moses and the children of Israel in one of my favorite Psalms:

Psalm 103:6 &7: *"The LORD executes righteousness and justice for all who are oppressed.* **He made known His ways to Moses**, *His acts to the children of Israel"* (Emphasis mine)

The children of Israel were more interested in what God (or Moses) could give them or do for them. They were more impressed with the power display of God through his servant, but were devoid of a sincere heart to pursue after the ways or righteousness of God. No wonder they were unable to sustain a lifestyle of faithfulness to God's laws and precepts, in spite of all the glorious works

> THE ONE WHO SEEKS HIS FACE WILL ALSO RECEIVE HIS HANDS

God wrought on their behalf and in their midst. On the other hand, Moses was more passionate and intent in knowing God and His ways, and thus He also had the privilege of not only exhibiting the character of God but also the one through whom God would exhibit His acts of supernatural power.

In summary, where as the children of Israel always sought the hand of God, Moses (and David) always sought the face of God. Let us always remember this truth: the one who always seeks the face of God (hungering and thirsting after His ways or righteousness), will also receive what is in His hands, being sustained by His righteousness and walking in His favor and power.

You and I have a choice to make. Will we rather be like the children of Israel, or will we choose to become like David and Moses? I choose the latter. Jesus made it clear, if we hunger and thirst after righteousness, (the ways of God,) we will be filled. Begin to hunger and thirst more after Him, and see your life transformed from glory to glory.

2 Cor. 3:18: *"But we all, with unveiled face, beholding as in a mirror the glory of the Lord, are being transformed into the same image from glory to glory, just as by the Spirit of the Lord"*

Chapter 5

MERCY: *Love's Language*

Blessed are the merciful: for they shall obtain mercy
(Matthew 5:7)

DAVID was a man after God's heart because he also understood more than any other in his generation how merciful God is; and by spending time in His presence this attribute also rubbed off on him. He knew how to pull the "heart-strings" of God. Even in the face of God's imminent wrath and retribution, David knew how to appeal to the mercy-side of God.

Such was the case when David sinned against God by asking his lieutenants to number the fighting men of Israel

(2 Samuel 24), as if his successes in military conflicts were as a result of Israel's manpower, and not by the outstretched arm of Israel's God. In view of this, God sent His prophet to give David His verdict. He had three types of punishment to choose from: seven years of famine in the land; three months of fleeing from his adversaries; or three days of pestilence in the land. David's response gives us insight into his intimate knowledge of God's character. He would rather fall in the hands of God, because of His mercy, than fall in the hands of man.

2 Sam. 24:14: *"And David said to Gad, "I am in great distress. Please let us fall into the hand of the LORD, for His mercies are great; but do not let me fall into the hand of man.""* (Emphasis mine)

Even though God still punished Israel for David's actions by unleashing a pestilence by the hand of an angel that killed seventy thousand men in a day, God's mercy was still kindled and caused Him to stay the hand of the angel from doing further harm. Instead of the three days appointed, the plague only lasted for a day.

We need to learn from this today as we witness devastating calamities in our society as a result of sin, that even in the midst of God's judgments, we can appeal to His mercy because He so much wants to release His mercy and blessing than His judgments. We need to pray like Habakkuk prayed:

Hab. 3:2: *"O LORD, I have heard Your speech and was afraid; O LORD, revive Your work in the midst of the years! In the midst of the years make it known; **In wrath remember mercy**"* (Emphasis mine)

God's nature has always been to project mercy rather than judgment. Even in the Old Testament where we witness how severe and unrelenting God's wrath and judgment could be against His own people, let alone His enemies; we can't help but notice that God much more enjoyed showing mercy more than executing His judgment. He reserved His judgment as a last resort after all else had failed to turn His people from their wayward ways back to Him. The Psalmist helps us to understand this:

Psalms 103:8 – 13: *"**The LORD is merciful and gracious**, slow to anger, and **abounding in mercy**. He will not always strive with us, nor will He keep His anger forever. He has not dealt with us according to our sins, nor punished us according to our iniquities. For as the heavens are high above the earth, so **great is His mercy toward those who fear Him**... As a father pities his children, so the LORD pities those who fear Him"* (Emphasis mine)

Once again it is important to reiterate that one of God's most pronounced character traits is mercy. God is LOVE, and mercy is love's language! One of the best places in scripture we can confirm this attribute of God as being one of His favorites is in Exodus 33. As I alluded in the previous chapter, Moses had just requested the Lord to show him His Glory. In response God tells Moses that He will let all His goodness pass before Him and then will proclaim the Name of the Lord (**Ex. 33:19**).

The Name of the Lord represents His character and attributes. This is very important because God was about to reveal to His servant what constituted His glory; which is who He is and what He has. I want you to pay

> GOD IS LOVE;
> AND MERCY IS
> LOVE'S
> LANGUAGE

careful attention to the very first attribute God introduces to Moses when He reveals Himself to him in the cloud of glory:

Exodus 34:5 – 7: *"Now the LORD descended in the cloud and stood with him there, and proclaimed the name of the LORD. And the LORD passed before him and proclaimed, "The LORD, the LORD God, merciful and gracious, longsuffering, and abounding in goodness and truth, keeping mercy for thousands, forgiving iniquity and transgression and sin, by no means clearing the guilty, visiting the iniquity of the fathers upon the children and the children's children to the third and the fourth generation.""* (Emphasis mine)

The very first attribute God wanted Moses (and us) to know about Him is that "He is merciful". Interestingly, the last item on the list is about His judgment, which though part of His nature, is the least of His attributes He likes or enjoys exhibiting. It is no wonder that God prefers to call His Seat the "Mercy Seat" rather than the "Judgment Seat";

and His throne-room the "Throne-room of Grace" were we obtain mercy, rather than the "Throne-room of Wrath".

God's Justice; God's Mercy; God's Grace:

There are three important attributes of God that I believe have been a source of misunderstanding in many circles, and even a source of controversy in others. They are God's justice, God's mercy, and God's grace. These three attributes of God are distinct from each other and yet interconnected and form the way God has dealt with and continues to deal with mankind in general and His chosen people in particular.

This is how one wise man explained these three attributes: "God's justice is when God gives us what we deserve. God's mercy is when God does not give us what we deserve. And God's grace is when God gives us what we don't deserve". In order to further explain, let us consider this illustration: Imagine a father gives his child specific instructions before leaving home for work and also specifically stipulates what the consequences would be if his instructions were not followed. The punishment would be one week of solitary confinement with no contact to the outside world, including no contact with any of the child's favorite toys. When he returns, the father finds that his child has violated all his instructions. If the father follows through and punishes his child to one week of solitary confinement, and does not allow the child to play with any toys; that will be justice. If he forgives the child and reduces the sentence to below seven days or even takes away the punishment all together; that will be mercy. But if he does not only forgive the child, but then also takes him or her out to go get ice-cream; that will be grace.

In His dealing with us, God's justice demands that we should be damned to an eternity separated from His presence in Hell because as the bible says *"all have sinned and fallen short of the glory of God"* (**Rom. 3:23**); and *"...the wages of sin is death..."* (**Rom. 6:23**). However, through the shed blood of His Son Jesus, He has forgiven us and rescued us by His mercy from our deserved punishment of hell. In addition, He gives us what we don't deserve; a new life full of His love, joy, and peace and furthermore an inheritance in Heaven: that is one important aspect of grace (unmerited favor)!

David, a Man of Mercy:

King David exemplified this process in his benevolent attitude towards Mephibosheth; Jonathan's son. After King Saul and his son Jonathan were killed in battle and David assumed the throne, he showed overwhelming benevolence to Jonathan's son that must have shocked many in his day.

Everyone must have expected him, after he assumed the throne, to go on a search and destroy mission to wipeout Saul's entire house in order to consolidate his reign. In fact, when Mephibosheth heard that the newly crowned king, whom his grand-father had sought to kill, had summoned for him, he expected as much. David would have been justified in taking his life; after all any other newly minted king would be expected to 'clean house'. However the opposite happened: not only did David extend mercy to this crippled son of his covenant friend Jonathan by withholding the sentence of death; he also showed him grace (unmerited favor) by inviting him to take a permanent seat at the king's table, just like one of his sons. In addition, David restored to him all the property that pertained to Saul's house, and assigned a servant to administer his affairs (**2 Sam. 9:1-9**).

What a wonderful picture of God's mercy and grace towards you and me administered through the death and resurrection of our Lord Jesus. We deserved death; but not only did He stay the execution, He also made us to sit together in heavenly places at His right hand and made us joint heirs with His Son, Jesus. And of course, He has also assigned His angelic messengers to minister onto us all the promises that pertain to our salvation, (**Heb. 1:14**).

Be Merciful:

This is the kind of attitude Jesus wants us to have when He talks about being merciful in His sermon on the mount. He is asking us to treat one another with the same kind of compassion David showed even his sworn enemies; and how our Heavenly Father also treats us. We are not to give people who mistreat us what they may deserve; which may be scorn, neglect, or withholding of our love. Rather we are to bestow benevolence to those who are in need but may be undeserving of our love. We are to walk in forgiveness, not holding people's faults and failings against them.

David was one of the most merciful men who ever lived. From his interactions with King Saul to his dealing with Mephibosheth and all his enemies, David proved himself to be a man of mercy and restraint. His interactions with King Saul epitomize this attitude rarely found in others. Even though Saul had every intention, and made every effort of eliminating young David from ever assuming the throne of Israel, after his own rejection from God, David never lifted his finger against his sworn enemy even when given the opportunity. Time after time

> LET MERCY ALWAYS PREVAIL OVER JUDGMENT AND RETALIATION

David spared the life of Saul, against the wishes of his own men, when killing him would have made his life more secured and his path to the throne more assured. On more than one occasion, God seemingly gave Saul up to David to execute; but on both occasions David refused to lift his finger to take Saul's life **(1 Sam. 24 & 1 Sam. 26)**.

I believe that the Lord put David in these positions to test his heart. Will he take matters into his own hands and requite vengeance and justice against his enemy? Or will he extend mercy and trust in God's judicial system and His faithfulness to fulfill His Word without man's help? When you and I are put in a situation where it is easier to pronounce judgment or enact revenge on an adversary, would we trust God and allow mercy to prevail over judgment; or let judgment and revenge take its cause?

I also believe that this attitude of David, to always allow mercy to overrule judgment, is the reason he also engendered so much mercy from God for his many shortcomings. He received so much mercy from God for his own attitude of mercy that God Himself associated His mercy with David, calling it "the sure mercies of David". This was a special kind of mercy God reserved for those who would walk like David in mercy towards others and therefore also receive the same kind of mercy David received from God.

Isaiah 55:3: *"Incline your ear, and come to Me. Hear, and your soul shall live; and I will make an everlasting covenant with you—* **the sure mercies of David***"* (Emphasis mine)

Acts 13:34: *"And that He raised Him from the dead, no more to return to corruption, He has spoken thus:* **'I will give you the sure mercies of David.'"** (Emphasis mine)

God's Requirement:

In the Book of Micah God clearly shows us what he requires:

Micah 6:8: *"He has shown you, O man, what is good; and what does the LORD require of you but to do justly,* **to love mercy***, and to walk humbly with your God?"* (Emphasis mine)

Jesus reiterated this point in His dealing with the Pharisees, who were more interested in enforcing the letter of the law than in projecting the true nature of the Father's heart, which was love. They walked around with a prideful and judgmental attitude towards those who didn't follow the minute details of the law, instead of showing mercy and embracing them into the family of Jehovah.

Matthew 12:7: *"But if you had known what this means, 'I desire mercy and not sacrifice,' you would not have condemned the guiltless"* (Emphasis mine)

As Christians, we cannot afford to have a pharisaical attitude towards the backslider or even the unbeliever. Our loving and merciful attitude will win them to the Lord faster and easier than our judgmental attitude ever will.

The Reward:

Jesus made it clear in the "Sermon on the Mount" that the reward for being merciful towards others is that we will also obtain mercy from God and from others. This reward simply follows after the "golden rule" which states "Do unto others what you would have them do unto you." In other words, if you want to be shown mercy (which we all do,) then you

FORGIVE OTHERS THEIR FAULTS IF YOU WANT TO BE FORGIVEN OF YOURS

must first learn how to be merciful. Which one of us can honestly say we don't need mercy, especially from our righteous God? If God was to requite His righteous judgment on us for every sin and fault we have, which one of us could stand His justice?

In my book, *"Lord Teach me How to PRAY,"* I explain in Chapter 6 where I discuss "The Prayer of Confession," that "forgiveness from God is the gateway through which all His redemptive blessings flow". Without forgiveness from God, our prayers are mere words devoid of any answers since our sin is what blocks the flow of God's response and blessings to us. That is why Jesus in His lesson to His disciples about prayer stressed the importance of them forgiving others their sin, if they want their Heavenly Father to also forgive them their trespasses.

In other words Jesus made the Father's forgiveness of our sins contingent on us forgiving others their sins. Jesus emphasized this truth when He told the parable of the servant who would not have mercy on his fellow servant who owed him little; when the king had forgiven him his enormous debt. The result was that the king rescinded his mercy from the servant and cast him into jail till he was able to repay all his debt. Jesus ended His parable by saying:

Matthew 18:33-35: *"Should you not also have had compassion on your fellow servant, just as I had pity on you?' And his master was angry, and delivered him to the torturers until he should pay all that was due to him. **"So My heavenly Father also will do to you if each of you, from his heart, does not forgive his brother his trespasses'""** (Emphasis mine)

According to the Lord, we determine how much of God's mercy we receive; by the same token of mercy we extend to others.

Matthew 7:1 – 2: *"Judge not, that you be not judged. For with what judgment you judge, you will be judged; and with the measure you use, it will be measured back to you"*

In other words, when we withhold mercy from our fellow man, we also alienate or disqualify ourselves from receiving God's mercy.

Do you want to live a blessed life where the mercies of God freely abound towards you? Do you want to experience "the sure mercies of David"? Then the only pathway God has made for you and me is that we become more and more "merciful", for then we will also "obtain mercy".

Chapter 6

PURITY: *Your Divine Power Source*

Blessed are the pure in heart: for they shall see God
(Matthew 5:8)

A PREACHER once said "God is absolutely powerful because He is absolutely pure". The purity of any substance is what gives it its true essence, weight, and value. In the world of precious stones such as gold, the karat of the stone determines its worth and value. The higher the karat, the more valuable the gold is. The different karats are simply the measurement of the extent of the purity of the stone. The less impurities the stone has, the higher the karat and therefore the more valuable the gold. For gold, 24 karat is the standard for the purest gold, hence anything less than that indicates the presence of alloys or impurities therefore impacting its worth or value.

Similarly, the different oils extracted from crude oil, through refining, determines its use and the power of the output it generates in the engine it is placed in. For example the combustion power that the jet fuel produces is greater than that of the automobile fuel. The jet fuel has a higher combustion power than the automobile fuel because it is refined at a higher temperature and thus can be considered as higher in quality or purity.

God's ultimate desire for His children is that they will become just like Him in holiness and purity. He is so pure that it is impossible for Him to associate Himself with impurity. He is absolutely light that no darkness can coexist in His presence. In fact the bible reminds us that darkness is unable to comprehend the light, (**John 1:5**). In other words His very presence obliterates any similitude of darkness and impurity.

Since He is holy, and we are not; pure and we are not; light and we are not, it is impossible to have fellowship with Him if we remain in our state of sin and darkness. This is why He admonishes us through the early Apostles, like Peter and Paul, for us to become like Him; so He can dwell in us and through us.

1 Pet. 1:15 & 16: *"but as He who called you is holy, you also be holy in all your conduct, because it is written, **"be holy, for I am holy.""*** (Emphasis mine)

2 Cor. 6:14 – 18: *"... Do not be unequally yoked together with unbelievers. For what fellowship has righteousness with lawlessness? And what communion has light with darkness? And what accord has Christ with Belial? Or what part has a believer with an unbeliever? And what agreement has the temple of God with idols? For you are the temple of the living God. As God has said: "I will dwell in them and walk among them. I will be their God, and they shall be my people." therefore "come out from among them and be separate, says the Lord. Do not touch what is unclean, and I will receive you." "I will be a Father to you, and you shall be My sons and daughters, says the Lord Almighty"*

It is imperative that we understand, especially in our current generation, that God cannot and will not compromise His standards in order to accommodate man's propensity for sin and darkness. That is why He has made every provision for us to become like Him and therefore, operate with His power as He does.

That is also the reason why Jesus was so furious and adamant with the religious leaders of His day, because even though they tried to uphold the external form of their religion, they totally neglected the most important aspect of their relationship with God; which is a sincere heart of devotion and purity towards Him. He railed most at their hypocrisy whereby they insisted on the outward expression

> GOD WILL NOT COMPROMISE HIS STANDARDS TO ACCOMMODATE OUR SINFUL DESIRES

of their faith reflected by the way they dressed, the way they washed their hands before eating, and even their commitment to pay their tithes. However their hearts, which is the seat of who we are, was filled with malice, jealousy, pride, lust, greed, and any other vile thought and intention. He chided them for trying to wash the outside of a dirty plate while leaving the inside as filthy as before.

Mark 7:5 – 23: *"... 'this people honors me with their lips, but their heart is far from me..."What comes out of a man, that defiles a man.* **For from within, out of the heart of men, proceed evil thoughts**, *adulteries, fornications, murders, thefts, covetousness, wickedness, deceit, lewdness, an evil eye, blasphemy, pride, foolishness. All these evil things come from within and defile a man"* (Emphasis mine)

The Day Jesus got Angry:

In Chapter 3, I alluded to the story of when Jesus entered into the city of Jerusalem riding on a donkey while people spread branches and clothing on the road for His triumphant entry. What occurred after this unprecedented welcome must have come as a surprise to many, especially the religious leaders who were already fuming about the rapturous reception He received from the people.

The first place Jesus went to after He entered the city was the Temple of God. This is significant because on His approach to the city, He had wept over it because of the city's lack of preparation for His visitation. He had been struck by how nonchalant and apathetic the city was about who He was and what His mission was, which was to bring them deliverance and salvation. As a result of them "missing their day of visitation", they would have to get ready for calamity and crisis.

Luke 19:41 – 45: *"Now as He drew near, He saw the city and wept over it, saying, "If you had known, even you, especially in this your day, the things that make for your peace! But now they are hidden from your eyes. For days will come upon you when your enemies will build an embankment around you, surround you and close you in on every side, and level you, and your children within you, to the ground; and they will not leave in you one stone upon another, because you did not know the time of your visitation. **Then He went into the temple** and began to drive out those who bought and sold in it"* (Emphasis mine)

I believe this is what the Lord is saying to His Church and His people as He draws near to our cities and nations. Just like it happened with Jerusalem, God intends to visit our regions with His Person, presence, and presents of His goodness and blessings. However, when He finds the city or nation unprepared for His coming, He immediately turns His attention to the

> THE CHURCH IS TO PREPARE THE NATION FOR THE COMING OF THE LORD

Temple or House of God (the Church) to see what is happening there. This is because God expects the Church to be in the business of preparing the nations, cities, or regions where they are for the ultimate return of the King of kings and the Lord of Glory.

When He also finds the church or the House of God unprepared, He takes her through the same process of cleansing and transformation He took the Temple on His arrival in Jerusalem.

Matthew 21:12 – 14: *"Then Jesus went into the temple of God and drove out all those who bought and sold in the temple, and overturned the tables of the money changers and the seats of those who sold doves. And He said to them, "It is written, 'My house shall be called a house of prayer,' but you have made it a 'den of thieves.'" Then the blind and the lame came to Him in the temple, and He healed them"*

There are at least three types of "houses" Jesus expects His House or Church to become in order for Him to successfully transform our regions into cities of refuge, praise, and glory. These three ingredients form the basis of the mission of the church. They are:

1. House of Purity (Vs. 12)
2. House of Prayer (Vs. 13)
3. House of Power (Vs. 14)

Before I delve into the details of the process Jesus took the House of God through, it is important to remind us that the "House of God" is not necessarily the building you and I congregate in weekly to worship the Lord. On the contrary it is you and I; and also the corporate Body of Christ. The Bible clearly states that our bodies are the

Temples of God or the House of God; and when the individual Houses of God come together we then form the corporate Body or the Ecclesia of God in regions and nations.

1 Cor. 3:16 & 17: *"Do you not know that **you are the temple of God** and that the Spirit of God dwells in you? If anyone defiles the temple of God, God will destroy him. For the temple of God is holy, which temple you are"* (Emphasis mine)

1 Pet. 2:5: *"you also, as living stones, are being built up **a spiritual house**, a holy priesthood, to offer up spiritual sacrifices acceptable to God through Jesus Christ"* (Emphasis mine)

Therefore, as you read about the various houses God intends for His church to be, I need you to first personalize them before extending them to the Body of Christ as a whole. We will work our way backwards as we discuss the process Jesus took the Temple on His arrival to Jerusalem in order to transform it back to its original purpose; and what He intends to do in us, who are His House, His Church, and His Bride.

House of Power:

God expects His church or house to be a 'house of power'; where deliverance and healing takes place. That is why in verse 14, He healed the lame and the blind in the same Temple that the religious leaders had turned into something other than its rightful purpose; thus fulfilling His original mission as enumerated in His first sermon in Luke 4:18.

Luke 4:18: *"The spirit of the lord is upon me, because he has anointed me to preach the gospel to the poor; he has sent me to heal the brokenhearted, to proclaim liberty to the captives and recovery of sight to the blind, to set at liberty those who are oppressed"*

This is what He expected to see when He entered the Temple and what He expects of His church today. That is what the early church was in the Book of Acts when as a result of the demonstration of the power of God, they were able to transform cities and bring a great harvest of souls into the Kingdom of God.

Acts 5:12 – 16: *"And **through the hands of the apostles many signs and wonders were done among the people**...so that they brought the sick out into the streets and laid them on beds and couches, that at least the shadow of Peter passing by might fall on some of them. Also a multitude gathered from the surrounding cities to Jerusalem, **bringing sick people and those who were tormented by unclean spirits, and they were all healed"* (Emphasis mine)

Acts 17:6: *"But when they did not find them, they dragged Jason and some brethren to the rulers of the city, crying out, **"These who have turned the world upside down have come here too"""* (Emphasis mine)

The First Century Church understood that in order to fulfill the great commission of propagating the Gospel to their known world, they needed to walk in the demonstration of the power Jesus promised to release upon them. Jesus promised them power; and the power they received on the day of Pentecost upon their lives and that of their generation caused them never to be the same. We have the same mandate and commission from God in our generation and we would do well to respond just like the early disciples did.

Acts 1:8: *"But you shall receive power when the Holy Spirit has come upon you; and you shall be witnesses to Me in Jerusalem, and in all Judea and Samaria, and to the end of the earth"*

God wants you and I today to operate like Jesus did, and like the Church in the Book of Acts did. He wants us to demonstrate His power beyond the four walls of our churches, because we are after all His house or Temple and His Spirit dwells in us just as much as He dwelt in Jesus and the early disciples. Someone might say, "…but those miracles were done by Jesus and the Apostles, and I am not Jesus or an Apostle". What would you then say about Stephen and Philip…they were not Jesus or Apostles? On the contrary, they were "ordinary" men like you and I who became deacons and yet demonstrated the power of God so much so that the religious community became agitated, and also an entire city was transformed.

Acts 6:5 – 8: "*And the saying pleased the whole multitude. And they chose Stephen, a man full of faith and the Holy Spirit, and Philip, ... **And Stephen, full of faith and power, did great wonders and signs among the people**"* (Emphasis mine)

Acts 8:5 – 8: "*Then Philip went down to the city of Samaria and preached Christ to them. And the multitudes with one accord heeded the things spoken by Philip, **hearing and seeing the miracles which he did.** For unclean spirits, crying with a loud voice, came out of many who were possessed; and many who were paralyzed and lame were healed. **And there was great joy in that city**"* (Emphasis mine)

If an ordinary deacon filled with the Holy Spirit can go to a city, preach the gospel and work miracles so that the whole city becomes joyful, you and I can at least carry the gospel, with signs and wonders following, to our schools and/or businesses and expect joy to be released there also.

A few years ago the Lord reminded me of the fact that I am now a representative and an extension of Jesus. He revealed to me that Acts 10:38 is true about you and me today as much as it was true of Jesus.

Acts 10:38: "*how God anointed Jesus of Nazareth with the Holy Spirit and with power, who went about doing good and healing all who were oppressed by the devil, for God was with Him*"

Just as Jesus the Man was anointed by God with the Holy Ghost and with power, thus enabling Him to accomplish all the signs and wonders He did, you and I have also been anointed by the same God with the same Holy Ghost and power. God, therefore, revealed to me that since Jesus was called "Jesus Christ" because He was the Anointed One, I could begin to see myself as "Alfred Christ" because I have also received His anointing to do the same works. In fact the believers in the early Church were first referred to as "Christians" meaning "anointed ones" in the ancient city of Antioch. This terminology was used in Acts 11 after the community in Antioch witnessed the acts and lifestyle of the believers there. You and I have been called by God to also become "anointed ones" or more appropriately "Houses of Power."

House of Prayer:

Before Jesus transformed the Temple into a 'House of Power', bringing the lame and the blind to be healed, He had to first transform it into a 'House of Prayer'. He was frustrated that the priests and scribes, who should have known better, had made the Temple into something other than what God intended it to be.

When He proclaimed that *"My house shall be called a house of prayer..."* (**Matthew 21:13,**) He was referring to Isaiah 56:5-7 where God clearly enumerated through His prophet what His House is supposed to be like.

Isaiah 56:5 – 7: *"...Also the sons of the foreigner Who join themselves to the LORD, to serve Him, And to love the* *name of the LORD, to be His servants— Everyone who keeps from defiling the Sabbath, And holds fast My covenant—Even them I will bring to My holy mountain,* **And make them joyful in My house of prayer.** *Their burnt offerings and their sacrifices Will be accepted on My altar;* **For My house shall be called a house of prayer for all nations "** (Emphasis mine)

I believe the church in general today is operating like the one Jesus encountered in the Temple. Even though we have a lot of different activities going on in the church, we lack the power the Lord promised us we would have and operate in, thus becoming a 'House of Power'.

It is interesting that it does not say His house will be a "house of preaching", or a "house of singing" or any such worthy or unworthy thing we may do in His house. We need to realize that God has not changed His mind about what His House or Church should look or be like. He still expects it to be a 'House of 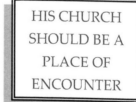 Prayer'; a place of encounter between humanity and divinity.

HIS CHURCH SHOULD BE A PLACE OF ENCOUNTER

Today the church puts more emphasis on so called "church growth" programs and principles; while prayer is left as an afterthought or relegated to a side room for only a special few. It is truly an indictment on the church when the prayer meeting is the least attended function or service of the church. No wonder we lack power to deliver a hell bound generation, who would rather seek out psychics and put their trust in the New Age Movement than in an impotent church.

If we want to become a 'house of power', we have to first become a 'house of prayer', because prayer begets power. Like the adage of old "more prayer, more power; less prayer, less power; no prayer, no power". We need to return prayer back to the forefront of our Christianity and church experience.

Once again, our ultimate example is Jesus Himself. In my book *"Lord Teach me How to PRAY!,"* I explain the reason why the disciples, given the opportunity to request anything from their Master asked Him to teach them how to pray (**Luke 11**). Even though they had seen Him perform miraculous feats such as healing the sick, raising the dead, feeding multitudes with few resources, calming

> THE SOURCE OF JESUS' POWER WAS HIS LIFESTYLE OF PRAYER

raging seas, and walking on water; their desire was that He would teach them the art of praying. This is because they understood that the source or secret of His power resided in His prayer life and communion with the Father.

Jesus began His earthly ministry in prayer, and ended it with prayer. You can go through the life of Jesus and come away astounded with His prayer life. He is either praying early in the morning (**Mark1:35**) or praying at night; many times ALL night. You ask "why don't we do what Jesus did (in terms of miracles)? The answer is: we don't do what Jesus did (in terms of prayer).

It is unfortunate that today, many Christians are pursuing the results rather than the source. We pursue power without prayer; we want Pentecost without the Upper Room; we desire fire without an altar. We have seminars and conferences on everything from how to grow a church to how to stay married; but how many seminars have you heard about or attended where they are teaching people not just how to pray, but to pray.

As important and urgent as the Great Commission was when Jesus commanded His followers to "GO", He knew that the commission would be without effect without the power of the Holy Ghost backing them up. We need to understand this truth: Jesus never intended for the Gospel to be preached without the power of God backing the message and the messenger up. In fact I dare say it is an affront to the gospel of our Lord Jesus Christ to preach the gospel without any power demonstrated to confirm the word preached. That is why in the same breath of urgency that He told them to "Go", He also told them to "Wait".

Luke 24:49: *"Behold, I send the Promise of My Father upon you; but tarry in the city of Jerusalem until you are endued with power from on high"*

The disciples waited in prayer for ten days before that day of Pentecost when a new dispensation and order was brought forth. It is amazing to note that Peter had been praying and fasting for ten days, and when the power came, he preached for only about ten minutes and saw over three thousand men convicted and saved. Today, most of us only pray for about ten minutes and wonder why it takes us about ten days of preaching or whatever else we do in the church to get three people saved.

Please don't settle for what passes for church nowadays. I believe you and I are part of the remnant church that God is raising up in these last days to recover what has been lost for a long time. We have to remember that the church was birthed in the crucible of prayer and power; it will only be sustained by prayer and power; and it will leave this earth in prayer and power. I am fully persuaded and convinced that we can have what Jesus had; what the early disciples had; and what our more recent fathers in the faith, like Charles Finney, John Wesley, John G. Lake, and Smith Wigglesworth, had. They had the tangible, unquestionable, undeniable presence and power of God as a result of their walk of prayer and intimacy with the Father. They were a "House of Power" because they were a "House of Prayer". You can have that too.

House of Purity:

Someone might say "but we pray at my church and yet don't see any power demonstration of the Holy Ghost". As much as that would be difficult to believe, since we know by biblical precedence, especially in the Book of Acts, that prayer always produced power; it goes to show that there might be a missing ingredient.

Before Jesus was able to transform the Temple into a 'House of Prayer', He had to first cleanse it from all its filth. He had to make it a 'House of Purity' before it could effectively become a 'House of Prayer'.

Before we also can truly become a 'House of Prayer', we need to first become a 'House of Purity'. It is purity in prayer that produces power. We need the Lord to come once again into His House and cleanse us and purge us of all our filth and impurities.

Someone might also want to know what really "ticked off" the mostly amiable Lord so much that He took out a whip and drove out these merchants out of the Temple; overturning their money-changing tables and opening the cages and stalls for the birds and four footed animals to flee. He then declared with indignation that they had turned His Father's House into a "den of thieves" (**Matthew 21:14**). What were they stealing? What was the big deal after all? In fact some might suggest that these merchants were rendering a very important spiritual service to those who came to the Temple to worship.

> PURITY IN PRAYER PRODUCES POWER

On the surface this might sound legitimate and worthy. After all, due to the nature of their religious worship and custom, every male was required to appear before the Lord at the Temple in Jerusalem to worship at least three times a year, (**Exodus 23:17; Deuteronomy 16:16**). The worshipper couldn't come empty handed as well, bringing with him the required animal, whether a lamb or dove depending on what sacrifice was to be made. However, due to the undue burden of having to carry the animal all the way to Jerusalem from wherever the worshipper was travelling from, a system of convenience was created in the Temple in order to help the worshipper fulfill his religious obligation without the extra burden. Thus, the business of trading was begun in the Temple where the worshipper would bring money, instead of an animal, and purchase the right animal at the Temple.

However, as it seems always is the case, this system became corrupted by the priests in the Temple who found a way to satisfy their greedy and racist hearts by "duping" the people of God. Firstly, the Priests who normally inspected the animals brought by worshippers to make sure it had no blemishes rejected a worshipper's perfectly unblemished animal. Since it would be too burdensome for the worshipper to return home for a new animal they would have to buy a new animal supplied and certified by the priest. The priest would then turn around and sell the same animal that was previously rejected to another worshipper. Hence with this practice, the priests were making untold profits, selling one worshipper's animal to another.

Secondly, since the worshippers only had the currency supplied and used by the Roman Empire, which governed the Jews during this time, they would have to change their currency into the Temple currency which was only available at the Temple. Hence, this trick gave the Priests another opportunity to rip-off the people by charging an exorbitant exchange rate. This was the purpose for the money-changing table.

However, the most sinister evil perpetrated by these Priests in the eyes of God I believe was that they were performing these actions in the area of the Temple that was especially reserved for the Gentiles who came to worship Jehovah. Therefore by setting up their merchandizing shop in this area they were depriving the Gentiles from having an encounter with God, which was God's desire for them. In the prophecy of Isaiah concerning the purpose of the House of God, God specifically made provision for the Gentiles who wanted to worship Jehovah in the Temple and also made sure that the priests recognized that it was a house of prayer "for all Nations"; not just for the Jewish nation (**Isaiah 57:5 – 7**).

As we can therefore ascertain, Jesus was not dealing with only the actions of the Priests, which might have looked legitimate, but more so with their wicked, corrupt, greedy, and racist hearts and motives. Jesus couldn't stand their corrupt minds and impure hearts and motives. The Temple needed cleansing and purifying.

Doesn't our Temple need the same kind of cleansing and purifying? Doesn't the church continue to have racist tendencies when Sunday remains the most segregated day of the week, and some people choose their place of worship solely based on the color or ethnicity of the Pastor? Doesn't greed and covetousness continue to be the motivation of some of our leaders, using God's name to make themselves wealthy at the expense of sincere but ignorant Christians? Don't we continue to harbor pride and lustful desires in our own hearts? We need to realize that until we are willing for the Lord to come into our

"Temples" and purify it we are going to remain prayer less; and therefore powerless. It is a true saying that "he who continues to sin will not truly pray and he who truly prays will not continue to sin."

Once again, it is purity in prayer that releases power, as confirmed also by James, the brother of Jesus:

James 5:16: *"Confess your trespasses to one another, and pray for one another, that you may be healed. **The effective, fervent prayer of a righteous man avails much**"* (Emphasis mine)

I absolutely love the Amplified Version of the bible which renders the last part of the verse thus, *"...the earnest (heartfelt, continued) prayer of the righteous man makes tremendous power available [dynamic in its working]"*. In other words it is the prayers of a pure man, woman, people, or church that makes tremendous power available to undo heavy burdens, destroy yokes, and bring souls to the cross of Jesus.

David's Pursuit of Purity:

David understood the relationship between purity and prayer so well. He knew very well that sin is always a hindrance and an obstacle to a true prayer life;

Psalm 66:18: *"If I regard iniquity in my heart, the Lord will not hear"*

That is why he also penned what I believe to be one of the most powerful messages in the word of God in regards to how purity and prayer in the presence of God releases the glory of God into regions.

Psalms 24:3 – 5: *"Who may ascend into the hill of the LORD? Or who may stand in His holy place?* **He who has clean hands and a pure heart,** *Who has not lifted up his soul to an idol, Nor sworn deceitfully. He shall receive blessing from the LORD, And righteousness from the God of his salvation"* (Emphasis mine)

David understood that God scrutinizes everyone who comes close to Him. It is one thing for us to ascend the hill of the Lord, but are we able to stand in His Holy presence? Anyone can approach the Throne Room of the Father but can we withstand the fire of His pure presence in the midst of our sin?

David makes us know that the qualifications needed to achieve a sustained encounter in God's presence in prayer are clean hands and pure hearts. Clean hands simply refer to our actions or inactions; while pure hearts refer to our attitudes and motives which may not be obvious to the human eye but are transparent before the fiery eyes of the Lord.

> SIN IS ALWAYS A HINDRANCE TO A TRUE PRAYER LIFE

It is noteworthy that after David discusses what it will take to be a passionate seeker of the face of God through purity and prayer, he talks about the King of Glory coming through the gates:

Psalms 24:6 – 10: *"This is Jacob, **the generation of those who seek Him, Who seek Your face**. Lift up your heads, O you gates! And be lifted up, you everlasting doors! **And the King of glory shall come in**. Who is this King of glory? The LORD strong and mighty, The LORD mighty in battle. Lift up your heads, O you gates! Lift up, you everlasting doors! And the King of glory shall come in. Who is this King of glory? The LORD of hosts, He is the King of glory"* (Emphasis mine)

I believe David was making a correlation between prayer and the release of the glory of God in cities and nations, culminating in the actual return of the King of Glory, Jesus, to the earth to establish His millennial kingdom and rule. Our prayers, done with clean hands and pure hearts, will open the gates and doors of our cities and nations for the revelation of the glory of God to be released. Church, we have a unique opportunity to partner with God through purity in prayer in the release of His glory, especially in these last days, before the coming of the Lord.

Habakkuk 2:14: *"For the earth will be filled with the knowledge of the glory of the LORD, as the waters cover the sea"*

With this understanding, that God uses our prayers done in purity to release His power and glory, David, who as we have already learned was a man after God's heart, pursued God with a heart of purity. He was not satisfied with a peripheral view of God but sought for a sincere and ongoing encounter in prayer with the One his heart and soul craved for. He knew that for him to continue to sustain a vibrant heart of fellowship with the Lord he needed also to maintain a pure and sincere heart. That is why one of his most urgent prayer requests was for God to continue to purge his heart of all conscious and unconscious sins.

Psalms 51:2 & 7: *"Wash me thoroughly from my iniquity, and cleanse me from my sin. Purge me with hyssop, and I shall be clean; Wash me, and I shall be whiter than snow"*

Psalms 19:12 – 14: *"Who can understand his errors?* **Cleanse me from secret faults.** **Keep back Your servant also from presumptuous sins;** *Let them not have dominion over me. Then I shall be blameless, and I shall be innocent of great transgression. Let the words of my mouth and the meditation of my heart Be acceptable in Your sight, O LORD, my strength and my Redeemer"* (Emphasis mine)

Psalms 139:23 & 24: *"Search me, O God, and know my heart; Try me, and know my anxieties; and see if there is any wicked way in me, and lead me in the way everlasting"*

Refiner's Fire:

As we mentioned in the beginning of this chapter, the way and manner precious stones, like gold and crude oil are purified is through a refining process. The process involves exposing the element to extreme heat. Since the impurities within the precious stone cannot withstand the high temperatures, they become separated and the pure product is therefore extracted.

In the same way, God takes us through His refining process in other to purify us by separating us from all impurities or sin. God is a consuming fire, the bible declares. What does He consume? Everything that is unlike Him!

Malachi 3:2 – 4: *"But who can endure the day of His coming? And who can stand when He appears?* ***For He is like a refiner's fire*** *And like launderers' soap. He will sit as a refiner and a purifier of silver;* ***He will purify the sons of Levi, and purge them as gold and silver, that they may offer to the LORD An offering in righteousness.*** *"Then the offering of Judah and Jerusalem Will be pleasant to the LORD, As in the days of old, As in former years"* (Emphasis mine)

The above scripture gives us a clear picture of the intent of God when we allow Him to purify us. His intention was that the "sons of Levi" who were the designated Priesthood would be able to offer onto God righteous offerings. In other words, their prayer (which was the primary duty of the priest) would be made much more effective due to their purified condition in God's refining fire.

The fire of God's presence obliterates everything impure that is exposed before Him. Since He is absolute light, no darkness is able to sustain long term in His presence. This should make you and I excited because we realize that God is not so much requiring us to purify ourselves outside of His presence, because we cannot. What He is requiring of us is to come and stay in His presence long enough, exposing all our weaknesses, filth, and sin in the light and heat of His loving presence and witness those impurities purged from our lives. In so doing we will become refined as pure gold, reflecting His power and bringing glory to His name.

1 John 1:6 & 7: *"If we say that we have fellowship with Him, and walk in darkness, we lie and do not practice the truth. **But if we walk in the light as He is in the light**, we have fellowship with one another, and **the blood of Jesus Christ His Son cleanses us from all sin"** (Emphasis mine)

The Reward of Seeing God:

According to the Lord Jesus, the reward or blessedness associated with pursuing a pure heart is "seeing God". I believe there are three dimensions to this promise:

1. Seeing God in Manifestation:

As I have previously stated, purity is God's power source. Hence, walking in purity allows God to manifest

Himself more in power in us and through us. In other words the more we allow our hearts to be purified the more we will see God demonstrate His power in answer to our prayers.

I believe this is the crust of what Jesus meant in His dialogue with His disciples in John 15. The whole purpose of abiding in Him is so that we will be purged in order for our prayers to be effective in bringing glory to the Father as we bear much fruit. I will repeat it again; purity in prayer produces power.

John 15:2 – 8: *"Every branch in Me that does not bear fruit He takes away; and every branch that bears fruit He prunes, that it may bear more fruit.* **You are already clean because of the word which I have spoken to you.** *Abide in Me, and I in you. As the branch cannot bear fruit of itself, unless it abides in the vine, neither can you, unless you abide in Me. "I am the vine, you are the branches. He who abides in Me, and I in him, bears much fruit; for without Me you can do nothing...**If you abide in Me, and My words abide in you, you will ask what you desire, and it shall be done for you.** By this My Father is glorified, that you bear much fruit; so you will be My disciples"* (Emphasis mine)

2. Seeing God in Circumstances:

It is not always easy to appreciate God in the midst of a negative and trying circumstance. We are often tempted to question where the presence of God is during our trial, and His purpose within it.

I have come to realize that the more I have allowed the Lord to purify my heart from my own selfish ways and desires, the more I am able to see Him at work even during the dark times of my life. I am able to have a perspective of the situation I couldn't have before; and this releases an attitude of patient endurance to deal with the circumstance with peace and joy.

When your heart is cluttered with your own evil desires and tendencies it is quite difficult to see God and serve Him faithfully when things and people are against you. You are quick to judge others and circumstances based on your own insecurities, bitterness, and offense.

Titus 1:15: *"To the pure all things are pure, but to those who are defiled and unbelieving nothing is pure; but even their mind and conscience are defiled"*

3. Seeing God Eschatologically:

Throughout the New Testament it is clear that Jesus is coming back for a spotless Bride. Many scriptures attest to the fact that purity and holiness are essential characteristics that will define the generation that will see the glorified Jesus in His triumphant return, and also define the Saints who will rule with Him in His Eternal kingdom.

Hebrews 12:14 – 15: *"Pursue peace with all people, **and holiness, without which no one will see the Lord**: looking carefully lest anyone fall short of the grace of God; lest any root of bitterness springing up cause trouble, and by this many become defiled"* (Emphasis mine)

1 John 3:2 & 3: *"Beloved, now we are children of God; and it has not yet been revealed what we shall be, but we know that when He is revealed, we shall be like Him, for we shall see Him as He is.* ***And everyone who has this hope in Him purifies himself, just as He is pure"*** (Emphasis mine)

This is why it is vitally important to revisit the "doctrine of grace" currently being taught in many circles that, consciously or unconsciously, refuse to put a demand on the listener to respond to God's love and grace by seeking to live a holy and purified life. Any message on grace that does not encourage you and me to respond to God in pursuing a life of holiness and purity is incomplete and can be dangerous.

As Paul aptly stated to His Roman hearers, God's grace is not our "permission slip" to live our lives as we please and expect no consequence from a holy and just God. On the contrary, grace is God's enabling power released into our hearts to influence us to think right and do right. Without the grace of God you and I will be hopeless in our desire to be holy before God. However, His grace has come

> GRACE IS GOD'S ENABLING POWER THAT INFLUENCES OUR LIFESTYLE

to teach and enable us to be godly; walking upright with pure hearts and clean hands.

Titus 2:11 – 14: *"For* ***the grace of God*** *that brings salvation has appeared to all men,* ***teaching us that, denying ungodliness and worldly lusts, we should live***

*soberly, righteously, and godly in the present age, looking for the blessed hope and glorious appearing of our great God and Savior Jesus Christ, who gave Himself for us, **that He might redeem us from every lawless deed and purify for Himself** His **own special people, zealous for good works**"* (Emphasis mine)

Hebrews 12:28 & 29: *"Therefore, since we are receiving a kingdom which cannot be shaken, **let us have grace, by which we may serve God acceptably with reverence and godly fear.** For our God is a consuming fire"* (Emphasis mine)

As Paul states to His protégé, Titus, the greatest purpose of the grace of God is to empower us to live godly lives now; and also prepare us to witness the glorious appearance of the King of Glory, Jesus, when He comes again to set up His eternal Kingdom on earth. If you pursue purity in your life, you will indeed see God!

Chapter 7

PEACEMAKER: *Like Father, Like Son*

Blessed are the peacemakers: for they shall be called the children of God (Matthew 5:9)

ALTHOUGH David was a mighty man of war, it is amazing to know that in his heart he was truly a man of peace. He fought and won his wars because that was his mandate and assignment from God in order to secure the peace of His people Israel from all their enemies, especially the Philistines. However, David NEVER held a grudge against even his worst enemies. He was always prepared to settle his differences and make peace with them if they were also willing. He never took vengeance into his own hands even when he had the reason and opportunity to. David was the ultimate human, peacemaker.

This attitude of David really baffled even his friends, and ruffled some of their feathers. They expected him to walk in bitterness and resentment against those who had made it their assignment to destroy him. In fact there were some who believed that they would obtain favor from him by doing him the "favor" of disposing his enemies for him. There are two instances of this.

Firstly, on the fateful day when Saul, who had purposed in his heart to kill David and hence had driven him into exile in the wilderness, fell on his own sword and died before the Philistines, a man ran to David to take credit for Saul's death. Instead of rejoicing, as others would over the news of the demise of his enemy, David instead went into mourning with all his men for Saul, Jonathan, and all of Israel. David then called the Amelikite, who came with an expectation of a reward; for after all he had killed David's enemy and now paved the way for David to take his rightful place on the throne of Israel. However, David's response to him was surprising, to say the least:

2 Sam. 1:14 – 16: *"So David said to him, "How was it you were not afraid to put forth your hand to destroy the LORD's anointed?"Then David called one of the young men and said, "Go near, and execute him!" And he struck him so that he died. So David said to him, "Your blood is on your own head, for your own mouth has* *testified against you, saying, 'I have killed the LORD's anointed.'''*

While David was made king over Judah in Hebron, Abner, Saul's Army Commander, had installed and propped up Ishbosheth, Saul's son, as king over Israel. The Bible makes us to understand that this was a tumultuous period in Israel's history because there were different allegiances; some were for David and others kept their loyalty to Saul. In fact the Bible says,

2 Sam. 3:1: *"Now there was a long war between the house of Saul and the house of David. But David grew stronger and stronger, and the house of Saul grew weaker and weaker"*

And so it was during this period that we witness the second instance where David took action against those who wished to procure his favor by eliminating his supposed enemies; found in **2 Sam. 4:1 – 12**. One day after the death of Abner, while King Ishbosheth took a nap in the afternoon, two of his lieutenants slaughtered him in his sleep and took off his head. They then came to David to express their allegiance to him with the head of his enemy in their hand. Once again, they assumed David would be favorable onto them but they did not consider what David had previously done to the man who claimed to have killed Saul.

2 Sam. 4:9 – 12: *"But David answered Rechab and Baanah his brother... "As the LORD lives, who has*

redeemed my life from all adversity, when someone told me, saying, 'Look, Saul is dead,' **thinking to have brought good news**, *I arrested him and had him executed in Ziklag—the one who thought I would give him a reward for his news.* **How much more, when wicked men have killed a righteous person in his own house on his bed?** *Therefore, shall I not now require his blood at your hand and remove you from the earth...* " (Emphasis mine)

David would not tolerate anyone who sought to secure favor from him by unilaterally eliminating his perceived enemies. He walked wholeheartedly according to the precepts and principles outlined by Jesus on the "Sermon on the Mount". He blessed his enemies; he had mercy on those who deserved to perish; he returned good for evil done to him, and above all he was a peacemaker.

David was ready to reconcile with Saul's House and even accepted a truce from Abner. This was a man who had pursued him with Saul to kill him. This was a man who had killed Asahel, Joab's brother and a relative of David. This was a man who was insincere in his loyalty to Ishbosheth, and only served him for his own gain. Yet, when he requested to see David, David threw him a party and dialogued with him about how they might unite and bring peace to the Kingdom.

2 Sam. 3:20 – 21: *"So Abner and twenty men with him came to David at Hebron. And David made a feast for Abner and the men who were with him. Then Abner* *said to David, "I will arise and go, and gather all Israel to my lord the king, that they may make a covenant with you, and that you may reign over all that your heart desires." **So David sent Abner away, and he went in peace"** (Emphasis mine)*

When Joab, David's Army Commander, heard that Abner had visited David and had been let go without any retribution for all his sins, he was furious at his master. Unlike David who was forgiving, Joab was a vengeful man who loved to settle his own scores. He sent back for Abner on pretense and cold bloodedly killed the unarmed man who believed he had received an assurance of peaceful relations from David and his men.

As you can imagine, David was not pleased with the actions of Joab, and actually pronounced a curse on him and his posterity.

2 Sam. 3:27 – 29: *"Now when Abner had returned to Hebron, Joab took him aside in the gate to speak with him privately, and there stabbed him in the stomach, so that he died for the blood of Asahel his brother. Afterward, when David heard it, he said, "My kingdom and I are guiltless before the LORD forever of the blood of Abner the son of Ner. Let it rest on the head of Joab and on all his father's house; and let there never fail to be in the house of Joab one who has a discharge or is a leper, who leans on a staff or falls by the sword, or who lacks bread.""*

119

David was so distraught with Joab's actions, that he asked all his men, including Joab, to mourn for Abner. He himself was the chief mourner following the casket of Abner with tears. He was crying because his former enemy was dead by cruel means, at the hands, no less, of one of his own confidantes, friends, and relative.

This attitude so endeared him to his people because they understood that it was never the intention of David for Abner to die such a "fool's death".

2 Sam. 3:33 – 39: *"And the king sang a lament over Abner and said: "Should Abner die as a fool dies? ... Then all the people wept over him again. And when all the people came to persuade David to eat food while it was still day, David took an oath, saying, "God do so to me, and more also, if I taste bread or anything else till the sun goes down!"* **Now all the people took note** *of it,* **and it pleased them,** *since whatever the king did pleased all the people. For all the people and all Israel understood that day that it had not been the king's intent to kill Abner the son of Ner. Then the king said to his servants, "Do you not know that a prince and a great man has fallen this day in Israel? And I am weak today, though anointed king; and these men, the sons of Zeruiah, are too harsh for me. The LORD shall repay the evildoer according to his wickedness."*" (Emphasis mine)

In this era, where it is common to hear people say, "My friend's enemy is my enemy"; isn't it remarkable to see

David lived the opposite of that? Do you rejoice when your adversary falls? Do you encourage others to do harm to your adversary or withhold good from them on your behalf? Do you seek revenge or retaliation for the wrongs that are done to you? Or do you rather pray for your enemies and seek to be reconciled, if possible, with those you have disagreement with? David exhibited and exemplified this beatitude to be a "peacemaker". No wonder he is known as the man after God's own heart.

Become a Peacemaker:

I believe it is easier to help make peace between two adversaries, than it is to make peace when you are the one who has been wronged. Being a Peacemaker means you are ready to reconcile others without being partial; but even more important being willing to reconcile with those who oppose you and even seek your harm. This takes a great deal of our ability, by God's grace, to walk in love, forgiveness, and meekness (humility).

In the "Sermon on the Mount", Jesus connected our ability to receive answers to our prayers to our ability to forgive others and securing a peaceful relationship with them. In the prayer He taught His disciples to pray, known as the "Lord's Prayer", the only portion He re-emphasized after the lesson was the part concerning forgiveness.

Mat. 6:14 – 15: *"For if you forgive men their trespasses, your heavenly Father will also forgive you: But if you forgive not men their trespasses, neither will your Father forgive your trespasses"*

121

In essence, Jesus is saying that un-forgiveness is one sure way not to have your prayers answered by God. In continuing with that same train of thought, He discussed how God views our spiritual sacrifices when we harbor un-forgiveness, resentment, and grudges against others. He said to His Jewish hearers at the time that they would have to reconcile with any known adversary before God would gladly receive their sacrifices; or prayers for us contemporary hearers.

Mat. 5:23 – 25: *"Therefore if you bring your gift to the altar, and there remember that your brother has something against you, leave your gift there before the altar, and go your way.* **First be reconciled to your brother***, and then come and offer your gift..."* (Emphasis mine)

The Bait of Satan:

In his book, *"The Bait of Satan"*, John Bevere aptly points out that offense is one of the devil's "most deceptive and insidious kinds of bait₃". It is the one effective way he uses to cause us to lose our vibrancy in our relationship and fellowship with God and our fellow man. Many marriages have ended in the divorce court because husband and wife were unable, or refused to let go of their offense. One or both partners refused to be the "peacemaker" in that relationship.

> OFFENSE IS ONE OF THE DEVIL'S GREATEST BAITS

There are Ministers of God who are leading congregations of hundreds and thousands who are ministering with offenses and grudges against other ministers. There are many also sitting in pews in our churches that refuse to let go of offenses against their fellow Christian brothers and sisters.

This unfortunate lack of a full pursuit and embrace of the beatitude to be a "peacemaker" in the Kingdom of God is the reason the Body of Christ in many regions, and universally as a whole, seems to be divided and splintered into denominations, sects, and cliques. This obvious scheme of the devil to bring schism into various levels of relationships, whether in marriage, ministry, or in the marketplace is a total affront to the will and purpose of God.

Churches have being split up; homes broken up; and companies destroyed because of various offenses among the various share-holders at different levels. This cancer of bitterness and offense has even decimated whole neighborhoods and communities; and can actually bring down a whole nation. It is the cause of racial and tribal tensions in many parts of the world, especially here in the greatest nation on earth- the United States of America.

It is sad that the many in the Civil Rights movement today in America seem more bent on rehashing old wounds and promoting racial strife than aggressively seeking and working for a culture of reconciliation. Don't misunderstand me here. I am not suggesting that we pretend that the history of slavery and segregation that my

African American brothers and sisters have endured never happened. Nor the fact that inequalities in various aspects of our current socio-economic order disproportionally affects the African American population. However, I believe the reason why African American communities are still struggling with poverty, depravity, and social disorder is that though slavery and segregation have been abolished, most African Americans, with the help of some of our religious and Civil Rights leaders, are still seeking justice in the form of reparations from human agencies, and continue to allow bitterness to fester in the hearts of even our children. By neglecting to focus our efforts in building bridges of hope, peace, and reconciliation, our nation is often thrown into racial conflicts bringing division among its populace. Jesus once announced that a kingdom divided against itself cannot stand.

The greatest thing that could happen in this nation, where race relations is concerned, is for the African American community to take the attitude of David as outlined above, or Joseph who was sold into slavery by his brothers and endured great injustice. However, through his trust in God, he found forgiveness in his heart and was reconciled back to his brothers (**Genesis 37 – 47**). Joseph realized that though his brothers meant it for evil, God meant it for his good; to make him their deliverer and sustainer. He looked to God for his compensation, and he received it. African Americans can take comfort, in spite of our horrible oppressive history, in the fact that just like Joseph God has a plan to use what the enemy meant for evil for our ultimate good. However, we must allow God to deal with, and heal our bitterness and resentfulness. We must then forgive and work towards reconciliation, and leave justice and reparations in the capable hands of God. It is time we become peacemakers!

(My good friend, Brondon Mathis, has written a must-read book on this subject of race and reconciliation called "Religion, Race, & Reconciliation". It can be purchased on Amazon.com)

Paul categorically stated what God's will is for you and me when it comes to living in peace with others:

Rom. 12:17 – 21: *"Repay no one evil for evil. Have regard for good things in the sight of all men. **If it is possible, as much as depends on you, live peaceably with all men.** Beloved, do not avenge yourselves, but rather give place to wrath; for it is written, "Vengeance is mine, I will repay," says the Lord. Therefore "if your enemy is hungry, feed him; if he is thirsty, give him a drink; for in so doing you will heap coals of fire on his head."Do not be overcome by evil, but overcome evil with good"* (Emphasis mine)

Heb. 12:14 – 15: *"**Pursue peace with all people,** and holiness, without which no one will see the Lord: looking carefully lest anyone fall short of the grace of God; **lest any root of bitterness springing up cause trouble,** and by this many become defiled"* (Emphasis mine)

The greatest obstacle to becoming a "peacemaker" is pride and an over indulgent attitude of upholding your rights in any relationship. If I really want to be a "peacemaker", I would need to give up my right 'to be right' all the time. I would need to humble myself, and extend my hand of reconciliation to my adversary.

Honestly, this is the attitude God Himself took in coming to reconcile with man, who had betrayed Him, and in essence had become His adversary. As we are about to see, that is why the reward or blessing associated with being a "peacemaker" is that you will be *called the children of God*"; or more accurately you will be called the sons of God.

Becoming Sons of God:

There are two terms the Bible uses in describing children of God. The first is the Greek word "Teknon" which means 'a child who is produced$_2$'. This term is more associated with being an offspring of someone or something. In other words, when a baby is born he or she is considered to be a "teknon", a child who is of the offspring of his or her father, but does not yet have the qualities, characteristics, or attributes of his or her father.

At a certain point in the child's maturity and growth when he or she begins to exhibit certain qualities, characteristics, and attributes of his or her father, the child is no longer called a "teknon" but a "uihos". This term, uihos, is reserved for those children who have matured enough to be now considered as sons.

Some scriptural references that use "teknon" instead of "uihos" to describe son-ship are:

John 1:11 - 13: *"He came to His own, and His own did not receive Him.* **But as many as received Him, to them He gave the right to become children of God,** *to those who believe in His name: who were born, not of blood, nor of the will of the flesh, nor of the will of man, but of God"* (Emphasis mine)

We see here that John refers to those who initially come to Jesus, receive Him as Lord and Savior are given the right or authority to become children or direct offspring of God (verse 13). This does not mean they become recognized immediately as matured sons but have begun the journey towards son-ship.

In fact, the Bible unequivocally describes who qualifies to be considered a son:

Rom. 8:14: *"For as many as are led by the Spirit of God,* ***these are the sons of God"*** (Emphasis mine)

In this verse, the word translated as "sons" is the word "uihos" in the Greek lexicon. Again this word is reserved for those 'children' who are matured and therefore are actually exhibiting certain characteristics and attributes of their Father.

This is the term Jesus used most often when He described His relationship with God, the Father. This often also got Him into a lot of trouble with the religious aristocrats of His day because they, more than the average person, understood the connotation when Jesus referred to Himself as the "Son of God". They were not mistaken in their understanding that Jesus invariably meant He was like the Father in all essential details and characteristics.

Jesus' most important assignment, beyond dying on the cross to redeem humanity, was to show us what God is like. If you saw Jesus it was as much as seeing the Father. That is why Jesus did not hesitate in telling His disciples that they had already seen the Father by seeing Him:

John 14:8 – 10: *"Philip said to Him, "Lord, show us the Father, and it is sufficient for us."Jesus said to him, "Have I been with you so long, and yet you have not known Me, Philip?* ***He who has seen Me has seen the Father****; so how can you say, 'Show us the Father'? Do you not believe that I am in the Father, and the Father in Me? The words that I speak to you I do not speak on My own authority; but the Father who dwells in Me does the works"* (Emphasis mine)

Jesus, therefore, tells us in the Sermon on the Mount that the one quality that will qualify us to be called the 'sons of God', having the Father's character, is being a peacemaker. After all that is who the Father is: a Peacemaker.

Ever since the fall of man when Adam willingly sided with God's arch-enemy, the devil, the Father has been going out of His way to make peace or reconcile with His creation, culminating in the birth, death, burial, resurrection, and ascension of Jesus Christ. The whole redemption story is about the God-Head seeking to reconcile with creation, man being the apex of that creation.

Col. 1:20 & 21: *"and by **Him to reconcile all things to Himself**, by Him, whether things on earth or things in heaven, **having made peace through the blood of His cross**. And you, who once were alienated and enemies in your mind by wicked works, **yet now He has reconciled***" (Emphasis mine)

You see, it is the Father's nature to be a peacemaker. The Holy Trinity doesn't know how to carry a grudge or offense against any one. God is love personified and one of the qualities we know about love according to Apostle Paul is that it does not get easily provoked nor does it think evil against any one (**1 Cor. 13:5**).

Just as God is a peacemaker or reconciler, that is what He has also commissioned us to be and do. He has committed unto us the ministry of reconciliation according to the Apostle Paul. This means not only is He asking us to reconcile or make peace with each other but also to actively participate in His mission to reconcile sinful man back to Him and in the end the whole creation.

2 Cor. 5:18 – 20: *"Now all things are of God, **who has reconciled us to Himself through Jesus Christ**, and **has given us the ministry of reconciliation**, that is, that*

*God was in Christ reconciling the world to Himself, not imputing their trespasses to them, and **has committed to us the word of reconciliation**. Now then, we are ambassadors for Christ, as though God were pleading through us: we implore you on Christ's behalf, be reconciled to God"* (Emphasis mine)

Rom. 8:19: *"For the earnest expectation of the creation eagerly waits for the revealing of the sons of God"*

What a blessing to be considered as a son of God because I exhibit His traits and characteristics. It is time to let go of our bitterness, offenses, and un-forgiveness and embrace wholeheartedly the nature of a Peacemaker. The whole creation is depending on it.

Chapter 8

PERSECUTION: *Don't Think It Strange*

Blessed are they which are persecuted for righteousness'
sake: for theirs is the kingdom of heaven (Matthew 5:10)

ONE of the most avoided subjects in the Body of Christ today, especially in the Western World, is the subject of persecution as part of the Christian experience. Many in the church today, aided along by preachers and teachers, eschew the fact that at one point or another they might have to endure persecution for the sake of Jesus and the gospel.

There are numerous scriptures that point to this truth, but many have been coaxed into believing that persecution for the believer is abnormal and even may be a sign of one's lack of faith. This cannot be farther from the truth; and yet it has lent itself to many unprepared but sincere believers who have had to deal with persecution in one form or another to stumble not knowing how to handle it.

It is also interesting to note that many who accept persecution as part of the Christian experience misunderstand what constitutes as persecution. Many Christians in the West think that giving up or being made to give up some comforts and conveniences for the "sake of Jesus" constitutes enduring persecution. Some see themselves as enduring persecution for Christ if they have to attend church on a cold winter day; or sit in a Sanctuary with no air conditioner in the heat of the summer; or sit through a two hour service on a hard seat without cushion for comfort. Others feel good about themselves if they have to miss their favorite show on TV in order to be in church or minister to a soul about Jesus.

All in all, the Western Church, like the Laodicean Church referenced in the Book of the Revelation, has been lulled to sleep by a gospel of convenience perpetrated by its preachers who refuse to put a demand on the people concerning their reasonable service as admonished by the Apostle Paul in Rom. 12:1.

Rom. 12:1 & 2: *"I beseech you therefore, brethren, by the mercies of God, that **you present your bodies a living sacrifice, holy, acceptable to God,** which is **your reasonable service.** And do not be conformed to this world, but be transformed by the renewing of your* *mind, that you may prove what is that good and acceptable and perfect will of God"* (Emphasis mine)

The sad thing is that this error is mostly begun from the onset of preaching the salvation message to the unbeliever. Most of our "altar calls" are essentially an invitation for the sinner to trade his or her "good" life for a better one. In other words we tell the sinner that if he or she accepts Jesus into his or her life, He would give them a better life, or make everything in their life better. He or she will have a better car, a better house, a better marriage, a better job...a better everything. And so with this in mind, the "poor" convert begins his or her Christian journey on a faulty foundation based on half-truths and unrealistic assumptions and expectations called faith.

Is it therefore surprising when this new proselyte, if not for the mercy and grace of God, becomes confused and sometimes offended at God when they suddenly realize that God is no Santa Claus. Along with that realization they begin to notice that the journey of faith is marked by pot-holes called tribulation, persecution, trial and temptations.

Are we also surprised at the state of our culture where even though many claim to be Evangelical Christians, there are nearly as much abortions committed among our ranks as in the general population, and the rate of divorce is the same if not higher in the church.

Due to our insistence on preaching this gospel of convenience, it is easier to compromise the clear standards of God's Word in the face of persecution, discomfort, and inconvenience; and sweep it effortlessly under the rug of grace, and conveniently say, "The Lord understands…"

We have to revisit the message of the gospel we preach, especially in the 21st century westernized church, and understand that giving up one or more comforts or conveniences for the sake of the Kingdom of God does not necessarily constitute persecution but rather is part of our reasonable service we render to the Lord in light of all He went through to procure such a salvation for us. We need to also understand that even though God is very much interested in the total wellbeing of His children, He never promised a life without tribulation and real persecution.

> GOD NEVER PROMISED US A LIFE WITHOUT PERSECUTION

Think It Not Strange:

On the contrary, He does promise us that we will have tribulation and persecution in the world. Jesus made it clear to His disciples then and now not only by this beatitude but throughout His life with them on earth, to be ready to face persecution and tribulation, with no exception. It was one of the last things on His mind just days before His passion to the cross, to prepare them of what was to come.

John 16:33: *"These things I have spoken to you, that in Me you may have peace. **In the world you will have tribulation**; but be of good cheer, I have overcome the world.""* (Emphasis mine)

The Apostles also, after enduring their own share of persecutions, never failed to remind those who came to believe on the Lord Jesus through them about the same admonition Jesus had given them before. From Peter and Paul to James, they all give a substantial amount of ink in their Epistles, supporting the fact that persecution for the believer should not be seen as a strange occurrence, but rather something to be embraced and endured because of the untold magnificence of the reward it procures for the believer now and moreover, in eternity.

The Apostle Paul, who endured so much persecution and peril after being responsible for the persecution of Christians himself, commended the Thessalonians for their endurance and patience as Emperor Nero was decimating the Church because of their unfeigned faith. He also encouraged his protégé, Timothy, to endure any persecutions that might come his way, (even within the church,) regardless of his youthfulness.

2 Thess. 1:4: *"so that we ourselves boast of you among the churches of God for your patience and faith in all your persecutions and tribulations that you endure"*

2 Tim. 2:3: *"You therefore must endure hardship as a good soldier of Jesus Christ"*

The Apostle Peter, I believe, has the most to say about the certainty of persecution for the Saint and how we should deal with it. First of all, he admonishes us not to think of persecution or trial as a strange occurrence for the believer, and then he encourages us to be joyful in the midst of our trial or persecution. Finally, and I believe most importantly, especially for those in the Western Church, he reminds us that there are many people around the world who are facing similar or worse persecutions than we are facing or going to face in the future.

1 Pet. 4:12 – 14: *"Beloved, **do not think it strange concerning the fiery trial which is to try you**, as though some strange thing happened to you; **but rejoice to the extent that you partake of Christ's sufferings**, that when His glory is revealed, you may also be glad with exceeding joy. **If you are reproached for the name of Christ, blessed** are you, for the Spirit of glory and of God rests upon you. On their part He is blasphemed, but on your part He is glorified"* (Emphasis mine)

1 Pet. 1:6 – 7: *"In this you greatly rejoice, though now for a little while, if need be, **you have been grieved by various trials**, that the genuineness of your faith, being much more precious than gold that perishes, though it is tested by fire, may be found to praise, honor, and glory at the revelation of Jesus Christ"* (Emphasis mine)

1 Pet. 5:8 & 9: *"Be sober, be vigilant; because your adversary the devil walks about like a roaring lion, seeking whom he may devour. Resist him, steadfast in the faith, **knowing that the same sufferings are experienced by your brotherhood in the world"*** (Emphasis mine)

Persecution: Don't Think It Strange

In many parts of the World today, Christians are in the throes of persecution for their faith. In the African nation of Sudan, for example, Christians in the South have been targeted for persecution by the more Islamic North. Husbands and fathers have been separated from their families and maimed or killed. Women have had their breasts cut off by machete and in many cases raped and sent into slavery all because they name the Name of Jesus Christ. Christians in Nigeria, Egypt, and Iran have also been brutalized and witnessed their church buildings burnt down.

Recently, a Christian Pastor in Iran was found guilty and sentenced to jail by the Islamic Court for strengthening the Christians there. This is not an isolated incident. There are many missionaries all over the world risking their very lives for the gospel's sake, reaching out to the un-churched and Christians in the underground churches in China and some parts of the Middle-East with resources; but most importantly with the power of the cross. Unlike the church in the West, these Christians and missionaries understand and appreciate what true persecution is. Even though many would prefer freedom from oppression and persecution for their faith, they also understand that it is part of the Christian "package" and enduring it has rewards only God can give.

A story is told of how a missionary from America visited the underground church in China and saw all that they had to endure in order to escape the wrath of the Communist Regime and still be able to worship the Lord. In spite of their predicament, these Chinese Christians have a vibrancy of heart toward the Lord more than most Christians in the West have sitting in the comfort of their padded pews underneath crystal chandeliers; without any fear of retribution. As the missionary prepared to depart from China, she sincerely showed concern for her Christian brethren and so offered to pray diligently for them with her friends upon return to the States that they will be relieved of their persecution. To her astonishment, the request was kindly rejected by the Chinese, but instead they offered to be praying for her and the Church in America. Their topic of prayer for the church in America would be for God to send persecution in order for the church to wake up from its slumber, apathy, and compromise.

Even though we in the Western Church may not be facing such persecution outlined above, although that is beginning to change as a result of ungodly legislations arising in many quarters to restrict the church from preaching the unadulterated Word of God, many of us still face persecutions for our faith in the public square whether in the home, work place, or schools.

Christians are ridiculed and marginalized in places like Hollywood and the political arena, especially if they refuse to compromise their beliefs and biblical standards. There are others who become victimized for promotions or salary increases by their superiors because they insist on doing the right thing before God's sight. A friend of mine actually had his employment terminated simply because he refused to lie on behalf of his supervisor who was engaging in an unethical act. There are many untold stories of Christian women not getting the opportunity they are well qualified for simply because they refuse to give in to the sexual advances of the man granting that opportunity. Our Christian children and students are sometimes persecuted in the schools by peers or even teachers because of their faith.

Unfortunately, due to the faulty biblical foundation many in our churches have, especially where persecution is concerned, many Christians have also succumbed to the pressures and persecution that has come their way. We have all probably heard of or know gifted Christian artists and athletes who could not withstand the pressures and allures of Hollywood, the NFL, or the NBA and are no more a vibrant witness for the gospel of Christ.

Ordinary Christian men compromise their biblical beliefs and convictions for fear of becoming unemployed and destitute. Sadly some Christian women, both single and married, have given in to the demands of men who are not their husbands against their better judgment for fear of losing out on an opportunity. While many of our Christian students have been able to stand firm on their beliefs, others have been swayed by the constant ridicule and persecution in order to conform and be accepted.

It is even more amazing that many Christians are persecuted by their own fellow Christians, who are supposed to be their brothers and sisters, for their vibrancy of faith; and passionate pursuit of wholehearted devotion to the Lord. It should not however come as a surprise because the Lord Jesus himself was betrayed by one of His own disciples, and crucified by the religious community at the hands of the Romans. The patriarchs of the early church were also mostly persecuted by the religious elites of their day because they were filled with the Spirit of the One they had crucified and were passionate for His cause. In fact, the very first case of persecution which resulted in murder occurred because Cain could not stand his brother Abel's wholehearted devotion to God.

As a Christian who desires to walk in full devotion and obedience to God, you should expect some fellow Christians who don't have similar aspirations to ridicule you for praying too much; fasting too much; giving or serving too much. They might even accuse you of being 'holier-than-thou' or a legalist. You may not be accepted in the fellowship because even though they might deny it, you bring a certain kind of conviction to their hearts for their apparent lack of wholehearted devotion to the Lord. Such was the kind of persecution King David endured from his own brethren.

David's Persecution:

As we know from the story of King David, he had a passionate heart towards God right from his youth. Even as a teenager tending the sheep folds of his father, David had a heart after God and had divine encounters with Him in the wilderness outside the view of the public eye. His devotion to God was personal, sincere, and passionate. His tenacious love for God helped to shape his world view of the supremacy and pre-eminence of God in Jewish culture and society. This is what caused him to be agitated when the army of Israel, including the king, shrank from the uncircumcised Philistines, led by Goliath who taunted them. His passion for God was so obvious it made his own brothers uncomfortable and jealous.

Even as the king of God's people, his passion for God did not subside but rather became part of his public persona. This passion and devotion to God also became one of the sources of his persecution throughout his life. His own wife was one of the first to criticize and ridicule him because he danced before the Lord with all his might in the view of all his subjects as he led the procession, bringing back the Ark of God into the city.

2 Sam. 6:14 – 22: *"Then David danced before the LORD with all his might; and David was wearing a linen ephod. So David and all the house of Israel brought up the ark of the LORD with shouting and with the sound of the trumpet. Now as the ark of the LORD came into the City of David, Michal, Saul's daughter, looked through a window and saw King David leaping and whirling before the LORD; **and she despised him in her heart**...And Michal the daughter of Saul came out to meet David, and said, "How glorious was the king of Israel today, uncovering himself today in the eyes of the maids of his servants, as one of the base fellows shamelessly uncovers himself!" So David said to Michal, "It was before the LORD, who chose me instead of your father and all his house, to appoint me ruler over the people of the LORD, over Israel. Therefore I will play music before the LORD. And I will be even more undignified than this, and will be humble in my own sight. But as for the maidservants of whom*

you have spoken, by them I will be held in honor."'
(Emphasis mine)

David, even as a king, endured persecution as a result of his uncompromising loyalty to God and passionate pursuit of His righteousness. He understood that many of the reproaches he bore from his own brethren were as a result of his passionate pursuit of the presence of God in fasting and prayer.

Psalms 69:6 – 12: *"Let not those who wait for You, O Lord GOD of hosts, be ashamed because of me; Let not those who seek You be confounded because of me, O God of Israel. Because* **for Your sake I have borne reproach***; Shame has covered my face.* **I have become a stranger to my brothers***, And an alien to my mother's children;* **Because zeal for Your house has eaten me up***, And the reproaches of those who reproach You have fallen on me.* **When I wept** *and chastened* **my soul with fasting, That became my reproach.** *I also made sackcloth my garment; I became a byword to them. Those who sit in the gate speak against me, And I am the song of the drunkards"* (Emphasis mine)

We understand and appreciate that this Psalm was also fulfilled by the Lord Jesus Christ. He walked in the footsteps of David, a man acquainted with grief and persecuted by His own brethren for His own passion to please His Father.

Inheriting the Kingdom:

In speaking about the blessing or reward associated with this beatitude, we once again see Jesus associating it to inheriting the kingdom of God as the reward. This buttresses the importance of this beatitude in the everyday living of God's people.

Since we have already discussed what it means to inherit the kingdom of God in Chapter 1, let it suffice us to say that as Christians especially in the West, we need to have our minds renewed concerning the subject of persecution. If we will inherit the tremendous blessings in the Kingdom of God now and in the age to come, we need to embrace the concept of enduring persecution for Jesus' sake. Especially in these last days when the enemy continues to inspire and influence leaders like the anti-Christ to enact laws which will inevitably result in the persecution of Christians who refuse to comply with the ungodly laws and norms of the world they live in.

Chapter 9

GIVING, PRAYING, & FASTING: *The Three Fold Cord*

IN the course of Jesus' Sermon on the Mount, He gives His listeners some nuggets of wisdom that if they would employ as part of their daily activities, they would be enabled to walk out the principles enshrined in the sermon. Among the many activities Jesus admonished His listeners to incorporate in their daily lives in order to effectively live the Kingdom lifestyle; three stand out to me: Giving, Praying, and Fasting. I refer to these as the threefold cord.

As I explained in the *Introduction*, these beatitudes espoused by Jesus, as the apex of our Christian endeavor with all its rewards, cannot be accomplished in our own human intellect, strength and resolve. They are characteristics and attributes of God that He graciously produces in our lives as we position our hearts constantly before Him and pursue these three activities. In other words, in order for the soil of our hearts to become tenderized enough to produce these fruits of righteousness, we must water and tend to it through giving, praying, and fasting.

It is important to note that when Jesus speaks about these three activities in Matthew Chapter Six, He does not discuss them as an "option" but rather as a compulsion or command. He uses the definite term "when" and not the conditional term "if" in discussing these three activities. This signifies that not only are they important to the believer's ability to grow in these beatitudes, but they are activities that he or she must do, without exception.

Giving:

The first activity Jesus speaks about is giving:

Matthew 6:1 – 4: *""Take heed that you do not do your charitable deeds before men, to be seen by them. Otherwise you have no reward from your Father in heaven. Therefore, **when you do a charitable deed**, do not sound a trumpet before you as the hypocrites do in the synagogues and in the streets, that they may have glory from men. Assuredly, I say to you, they have their reward. But **when you do a charitable deed**, do not let your left hand know what your right hand is doing, that your charitable deed may be in secret; and your Father who sees in secret will Himself reward you openly"* (Emphasis mine)

As we can see, Jesus did not make giving an option by using the definite term "when". Again, this means it is expected of us as those pursuing a wholehearted relationship with God.

Many in the Body of Christ have become suspicious and cynical to the subject of giving due to some of the unfortunate abuse some in the clergy have perpetrated with the issue of giving. Nevertheless, it is important for you and me to still honor the Lord by obeying His command to give, irrespective of what others might say or do with this issue. The Apostle Paul reminds us how much more blessed it is to give than to receive.

Acts 20:35: *"I have shown you in every way, by laboring like this, that you must support the weak. And remember the words of the Lord Jesus, that He said, '**It is more blessed to give than to receive.**' "* (Emphasis mine)

Giving is such a fundamental aspect of the Godhead. Like we have said a few times already, God does not tell us to do something He Himself hasn't already done or is doing. God tells us to give because He has already given His best to us and continuous to give us our hearts desires according to His will. It is therefore a privilege to partake in the Father's nature by becoming a giver.

John 3:16: *"For God so loved the world that **He gave His only begotten Son**, that whoever believes in Him should not perish but have everlasting life"* (Emphasis mine)

Rom. 8:32: *"He who did not spare His own Son, but delivered Him up for us all, how shall He not with Him **also freely give us all things?**"* (Emphasis mine)

When we give to others with a sincere and genuine heart; of our time or resources such as money, possessions, gifting and/or talents; we also position ourselves to receive from God and others. This attitude of giving also confirms and strengthens our resolve to walk in meekness and humility as we use our resources to serve God's purposes in the lives of others. May God grant you the grace of giving, so that through your heart of giving, He will speak well of you and also release resources into your life for Kingdom advancement.

2 Cor. 9:6 – 8: *"But this I say: He who sows sparingly will also reap sparingly, and he who sows bountifully will also reap bountifully. So **let each one give as he purposes in his heart**, not grudgingly or of necessity; **for God loves a cheerful giver. And God is able to make all grace abound toward you, that you, always having all sufficiency in all things, may have an abundance for every good work**"* (Emphasis mine)

Praying:

The second activity Jesus mentioned for us to incorporate into our daily lives to enable us live the Kingdom lifestyle He espoused on the 'Sermon on the Mount' is prayer. Once again, note the definite term "when" and not the conditional term "if," that he associates with this activity.

Matthew 6:5 & 6: *""And **when you pray,** you shall not be like the hypocrites. For they love to pray standing in the synagogues and on the corners of the streets, that they may be seen by men. Assuredly, I say to you, they have their reward. **But you, when you pray,** go into your room, and when you have shut your door, pray to your Father who is in the secret place; and your Father who sees in secret will reward you openly"* (Emphasis mine)

Instead of spending much time on this subject of prayer, of which I have a lot to say about its importance to the child of God; I would rather recommend that you read my book solely dedicated to the subject of prayer, *"Lord Teach me How to PRAY!"* (It can be purchased on amazon.com or www.alfredtagoe.webs.com).

Prayer is as vital to the life of the believer as air is to the life of everyone. Without this activity becoming a pervading influence in our lives, we become virtually lifeless spiritually and hence not possible to live out these principles and attitudes espoused by Jesus in His sermon. In other words, prayer opens up our spiritual respiratory system to effectively inhale the grace of God; and exhale the life of God as evidenced by our lifestyle based on the "Sermon on the Mount" mindset. The father of the Methodist movement, John Wesley, put it succinctly in this way; "Ask [pray], that you may thoroughly experience and perfectly practice the whole of that religion that our Lord has so beautifully described in the Sermon on the Mount₄" So why don't you begin a new journey and lifestyle of prayer?

We are admonished by the Lord Jesus that *"men ought always to pray and not to faint"* (**Luke 18:1**). In other words, if you sense you are fainting in your ability to please God as you endeavor to walk out these beatitudes in your life, it must mean that you are attempting to accomplish it without the precious resource of prayer. I like to say it this way, "if you are praying, you are not fainting; and if you are fainting, you must not be praying". Start praying today and see the Lord release His grace and strength into your life like He did for Jesus and the First Century disciples.

Fasting:

The third activity Jesus admonished His listeners to engage in is fasting. We once again see the use of "when", and not "if", in association with this activity; indicating that it is not optional but compulsory for the Saint.

Mat. 6:16 – 18: *""Moreover, **when you fast**, do not be like the hypocrites, with a sad countenance. For they disfigure their faces that they may appear to men to be fasting. Assuredly, I say to you, they have their reward. **But you, when you fast**, anoint your head and wash your face, so that you do not appear to men to be fasting, but to your Father who is in the secret place; and your Father who sees in secret will reward you openly"* (Emphasis mine)

Once again, instead of using this forum to write an in depth study on the subject of fasting, as important and sometimes controversial in certain circles as it is, I will recommend the book, *"The Rewards of Fasting"* by Mike

Bickle and Dana Candler *(Can be purchased from www.mikebickle.org).* Even though there are other great resources that you may find on this subject, this book in my opinion gives the most in-depth and yet balanced approach to biblical fasting that I have come across.

In brevity, however, we need to understand that God uses our fasting; done always in concert with prayer, as a catalyst to achieve His Kingdom purposes. In other words, adding a lifestyle of fasting to your lifestyle of praying quickens the process by which certain things are accomplished in and through your life. In fact, in one of Jesus' greatest statements concerning fasting, Jesus attributed the inability of His disciples to cast out a demon out of a young lad to their lack of fasting coupled with prayer.

Mat. 17:19 – 21: *"Then the disciples came to Jesus privately and said, "Why could we not cast it out?" So Jesus said to them, "Because of your unbelief; for assuredly, I say to you, if you have faith as a mustard seed, you will say to this mountain, 'Move from here to there,' and it will move; and nothing will be impossible for you. However, **this kind does not go out except by prayer and fasting.**""* (Emphasis mine)

This goes to show that prayer, as powerful as it is, is not always enough on its own to accomplish certain spiritual tasks. This includes our ability to live out the kingdom lifestyle espoused by Jesus on the "Sermon on the Mount". We need to incorporate biblical fasting, which includes but is not limited to the abstinence from food for certain periods of time, to our lifestyle of prayer. This speeds up the process by which your heart becomes tenderized enough to the point you are willing and able to fully obey the Lord.

I encourage you to endeavor to begin to live a fasted lifestyle; which means fasting becomes a daily or weekly lifestyle routine, (as the grace of God enables you,) rather than a once in awhile event in your life. Taking time to fast and pray once or twice a week will go a long way for you to see substantial victories in your pursuit of wholehearted obedience to God, more than a forty day fast once in a long while; even as important and laudable as that is.

Everyone in the Bible, like Moses, David, Jesus and Paul, who incorporated these three activities in their lives were not only able to live a vibrant lifestyle of obedience to God but were also used mightily to transform their generation for the Kingdom of God. Even an unbeliever like Cornelius who sincerely pursued a relationship with Jehovah received a divine visitation from the Arch-angel Gabriel and also the blessing of becoming the first Gentile to receive the promise of the Holy Spirit. All this happened because he applied the threefold cord of giving, praying, and fasting as the cornerstones of His pursuit of God. For that, a memorial was erected in heaven on His behalf; and for him you and I have to be thankful because he opened the door for us who were Gentiles to become engrafted to the stalk of Israel.

Acts 10:1 – 4: *"There was a certain man in Caesarea called Cornelius, a centurion of what was called the*

Italian Regiment, a devout man and one who feared God with all his household, **who gave alms generously to the people, and prayed to God always.** *About the ninth hour of the day he saw clearly in a vision an angel of God coming in and saying to him, "Cornelius!" And when he observed him, he was afraid, and said, "What is it, lord?"* **So he said to him, "Your prayers and your alms have come up for a memorial before God"** (Emphasis mine)

Do you sincerely endeavor to enjoy life in the Kingdom based on the "Sermon on the Mount" perspective? Do you want to have an impact in this world and in the one to come, as you live this Kingdom lifestyle? Do you sincerely want to be poor in spirit; mourn over your sins and that of your community and nation; serve God and people with meekness; hunger and thirst after righteousness; walk in purity; be a peacemaker; and endure persecution? If your answer is "Yes", then you have no choice but to have a fresh perspective on incorporating giving, praying, and fasting into your daily life.

May the Lord strengthen you and help you to enjoy life in His Kingdom based on the "Sermon on the Mount" perspective.

The Blessed Life

Footnotes

1. The Blessing of the Lord. By Kenneth Copeland. Published by Kenneth Copeland Publications (2011)
2. Strong's Hebrew and Greek Exhaustive Concordance and Dictionary. By James Strong (1890)
3. The Bait of Satan. By John Bevere. Published by Charisma House (2011)
4. Answered Prayer. By E. M. Bounds. Published by Whitaker House (1994)

Biography

Alfred Tagoe is the founder of *Voice of Revival Ministries*, a non-denominational prayer ministry focused on bringing a genuine Revival to the Body of Christ through prayer and the Word of God. As part of his mandate from God, he directs the *Columbus House of Prayer (CoHOP)*, a Prayer, Worship, and Justice center where believers from every denomination and ethnic background come and contend for the Heart of God through day and night worship and prayer to bring regional transformation to our cities and nation (Is 56:7). He also hosts Prayer Summits which call the Body of Christ to a "solemn assembly" to cry before the Lord on behalf of our land that it will be healed (Joel 2:15). Finally, through the *Nehemiah Project*, he has been uniquely called and gifted apostolically to bring the message of prayer and revival to Churches and Regions to 'rebuild the walls and repair the gates' of our cities the glory of God to be revealed (Neh 2:5).

Alfred has served in many leadership roles, especially in the area of prayer, ever since God birthed a spirit of prayer and revival in his heart in 1994. He is a graduate of World Harvest Bible College with a diploma in Pastoral Studies; and Franklin University with a Bachelor of Science in Organizational Communication.

His passion is to witness the last great awakening and revival; and help the Body of Christ rediscover their original purpose of intimacy with their creator God. His mission is to be a "forerunner" like John the Baptist to "prepare the way of the Lord" (Luke 3:4) and "make ready a people prepared for the Lord" (Luke 1:17). Alfred currently resides in Columbus, Ohio with his lovely wife Angelina and three children Jezaniah, Jaeda, and Joshua

Contact Information:

For more information about the Author, please write to:

Alfred Tagoe,
Voice of Revival Ministries,
5696 Earnings Dr,
Columbus Ohio, 43232.

Tel: 614-312-2624
Email: alfredchrist01@gmail.com
www.facebook.com/alfred.christ
www.voiceofrevival.net

For more information about the *Columbus House of Prayer (CoHOP)*, please visit website at *www.columbushop.org*
Or write to:

Alfred Tagoe,
Columbus House of Prayer (CoHOP),
1673 Karl Court,
Columbus Ohio, 43229

Tel: 614-5COHOP8 (614-526-4678)
Email: Director@columbushop.org

159

The Blessed Life

Other book by author on Amazon.com

The Blessed Life